Anselm Böhmer, Götz Schwab, Illie Isso (eds.)
Digital Teaching and Learning in Higher Education

Pedagogy

Anselm Böhmer (Prof. Dr.), born in 1968, is professor of General Education at Pädagogische Hochschule Ludwigsburg (Germany). He previously held professorships in Social Work and was a visiting scholar at the University of South Australia, Adelaide in 2015. His research focuses on education theory in late modernity, poststructuralist approaches of subjectivation, education and social differences, diversity, migration, culturalization, and digitalization.

Götz Schwab, born in 1967, is a professor of applied linguistics at the Institute of English, Pädagogische Hochschule Ludwigsburg, Germany. He is head of the institute and coordinates a number of transnational projects. His research interests include Conversation Analysis for Second Language Acquisition (CA-SLA), telecollaboration and the use of mobile technology, syntax, low achievers, and students-at-risk, ELT/FLT methodology in primary and secondary schools as well as Content and Language Integrated Learning (CLIL).

Illie Isso, born in 1982, has been a PhD student and research assistant at the Pädagogische Hochschule Ludwigsburg, Germany, since 2021 and is responsible for project management in both the Diva project and the new EUGEN project. Previously, he completed his teacher training in the subjects of history, ethics, technology and sport with the first state examination. His research interests include history, education and social inequality, diversity, inclusion and migration.

Anselm Böhmer, Götz Schwab, Illie Isso (eds.)

Digital Teaching and Learning in Higher Education

Culture, Language, Social Issues

[transcript]

Bibliographic information published by the Deutsche Nationalbibliothek

The Deutsche Nationalbibliothek lists this publication in the Deutsche Nationalbibliografie; detailed bibliographic data are available in the Internet at http://dnb.d-nb.de

First published in 2024 by transcript Verlag, Bielefeld
© **Anselm Böhmer, Götz Schwab, Illie Isso (eds.)**

Cover layout: Maria Arndt, Bielefeld

https://doi.org/10.14361/9783839462768
Print-ISBN: 978-3-8376-6276-4
PDF-ISBN: 978-3-8394-6276-8
ISSN of series: 2703-1047
eISSN of series: 2703-1055

Contents

Empirical Findings

Teaching Practices

Preface

Anselm Böhmer, Götz Schwab, & Illie Isso

Many stakeholders have been promoting globalization and transnational collaboration among researchers and students for many years. When the Covid-19 pandemic hit the world, digital literacy became crucial and was further developed to provide more, if not new, answers to the emerging challenges. Thus, virtual mobility became of paramount importance for higher education to respond to the new demands and conditions of the pandemic.

In 2020, an international research and teaching collaboration project, »Digital and International Virtual Academic Cooperation« (DIVA), was launched to promote the virtual mobility of students through blended mobility and blended learning.[1] Scholars from the participating universities in Israel, Australia, and Germany collaborated to focus on intercultural learning and online collaboration. In particular, teaching formats such as digital learning, peer learning, virtual cooperation formats for students and teachers, etc., were used and established. Based on the results of this project, this book discusses how such arrangements can be used in university teaching, how digital teaching can be theorized and conceptualized, and what potential it provides for future teaching in higher education after the pandemic. Our findings comprise an in-depth look at how global collaboration became intercultural learning for both students and faculty.

It has often been suggested that valuable lessons in digital citizenship were fostered during the pandemic. In particular, digital tools and skills were used in many ways (Schwab et al., 2022). So far, much has been written about the concrete practices, issues, process formations, limitations, and constraints – and the evidence-based consequences for further digital teaching in (higher) education (e.g., among many others Anthonysamy et al., 2021;

---

[1] This project was funded by the German Academic Exchange Service (DAAD), Project ID 57564212.

Böhmer et al., 2022; Petronzi & Petronzi, 2021; Waldman et al., 2019). Our book builds on these findings, reporting data and perspectives from our trilateral collaborative project on intercultural awareness in teacher education for global digital citizenship. We highlight conceptualizations of cultural differences, language competence, and social constraints on access, pedagogical practices, and consequences in emerging student-teacher collaborations. In pursuance of these goals, various theoretical underpinnings are discussed, empirical findings are presented, and various cultural, linguistic, and social differences are examined.

A coherent body of theory on digital teaching, its outcomes, and possibilities is still lacking to reflect the findings and structural foundations of the project. Thus, our book presents teaching and research findings to further contribute to a theory of digital teaching. We present and discuss our empirical findings, integrate them into existing theoretical frameworks, and enquire into conceptual consequences for teaching, research, and educational policy. In doing this, we provide practical insights into the processes, efforts, and factors that support digital teaching and learning. We take account of the different perspectives of the participating national education systems, but also consider those of other status groups such as scholars and students. In this way, we provide a multi-perspective view of what has happened, what has worked well and what has not, and how further approaches might be discussed. We also discuss misleading steps and concepts to better understand digital processes in higher education.

Thus, we aim to provide further insights into learning for post-pandemic teaching, such as those involving concepts of distance and/or blended learning and multi-perspective approaches to learning environments. We aim also to provide university teachers with better knowledge about learning for international collaboration, such as that relating to cultural ties, language ties and limitations, and social aspects of access and segregation in higher education. In promoting understanding of these aspects, our volume presents insights into learning in formal and informal teaching and learning settings.

All in all, our volume combines many different approaches and shows a great number of the relevant aspects of our project – and in the field of digital learning does so with respect to varying cultural foundations. We present papers that reflect on conceptualizations of communication (Albers et al.), cultural competence (Mason et al.) and culturally informed reflections on power for the »new normal« of digital teaching (Bolaji) as well as embodiment (Böhmer) as challenges for digital teaching in general. Our volume also refers to empirical findings on inter- and transcultural Experiences (Topaz et al.) and on telecollaboration (Meier), learning experiences in higher education (Krüger), and with peers in digital settings (Tripura Sundari & Wang). In this vein, the papers presented here provide helpful insights into the following aspects:

In the first contribution to this anthology, *Stine Albers, Bettina Blanck, Sarah Gaubitz, Viktoria Rieber*, and *Anja Vocilka* ask: How can concepts unfold in digital teaching and learning structures in the field of higher education? And what potential do creative debates have in the field of conceptual clarification work in teaching and learning? The authors consider these and other questions in their contribution »Working on Concepts as an Element of Communication and Starting Point for Research-based Learning in Higher Education«.

»Problematising ›Cultural Competence‹ in the Digital Environment«, *Jon Mason, Karen Cieri, & Chris Spurr* address an identified terminology problem of the term »cultural competence« in the research literature in the context of the rapidly evolving digital teaching and learning environment in the 21st century. In their article, they do not restrict themselves to the problematisation of prevailing culturally specific terms and definitions, but elaborate an alternative terminology that could guide future dialogues. The focus on »intercultural responsiveness« is a promising first step.

Although it seems that the limitations imposed by the COVID-19 pandemic have become an issue of the past, they nonetheless changed much of the reality in university teacher education institutions semi-permanently into a »new normal«. *Stephen D. Bolaji* shows in his contribution »Digitocracy in the New Normal: Rethinking the Learning Spaces in Higher Education« that this new normal is permeated by the approach of digitocracy. Against this backdrop, the author argues that the new normal should be understood as a challenge that needs to be considered in the higher education system – and in the social, intercultural and academic structures there.

Entitled »Digital Bodies – On Signification, Learning, and Embodiment in Digital Teaching«, *Anselm Böhmer*'s paper addresses questions about the bodily »habitus« in the context of culturalisation and digitalisation. More specifically, he relates the concept of embodiment – that is, the performance that requires a body – to the learning and teaching digital body. This critical reflection leads him to the challenging question of how future – digital – higher education could be conceived.

Beverley Topaz, Tina Waldman and *Götz Schwab*, look at the DIVA project mentioned above from a different perspective. In their chapter entitled »Inter-and Transcultural Experience among Future Foreign Language Educators:

International Virtual Exchange between Teacher Training Institutions«, they provide insight into their – data-based – experiences in areas of virtual exchange and inter- and transcultural learning. They not only illustrate that prospective foreign language teachers – despite various challenges – develop a collective professional identity across national borders, but also outline a newly developed more inclusive pedagogy.

The digital university reality during the COVID-19 pandemic is also relevant for *Svenja Meier*'s contribution. In her article »Personal Interlocution in Telecollaboration: Cultural Discourse Analysis of German and Israeli Teachers in Training« she deals with the individual narratives and representations of international student teachers in digital space. To do this, she chooses the approach of cultural discourse analysis, which she applies to analyse students' self-disclosures – that were recorded as part of the international project DIVA. Among other things, she shows that access to personal narratives – especially in a telecollaborative teaching and learning environment – can be a possible way to address and understand discourses in the context of culture and language.

Michael Krüger's chapter »Sense-making in the production process of online learning materials« highlights challenges and opportunities that have emerged in the IDEN (International Digital Education Network) project, a further research endeavour closely connected to DIVA. He thus provides important insights into a collaboratively developed asynchronous online learning model, which at its core represents a production process that both relieves lecturers partly of their customary burdens and enriches students.

This anthology is rounded off by a collaborative chapter by two participating students, thus creating a deliberate and important conclusion. The two contributions »A world of tomorrow. The perspectives of online learners on digital teaching and learning« by *Lalitha Tripura Sundari* and »How to facilitate peer interactions in virtual intercultural learning: an example in the DIVA project« by *Xirui Wang* are framed and contextualised by *Anselm Böhmer*. The reflections of both students provide an opportunity to look at the DIVA project in particular and digital higher education in intercultural cooperation in general from a student perspective, to evaluate it and to make it fruitful for future international projects.

In summary, we can say that this volume presents new insights into a field that has already been the subject of research for a considerable time. These are insights that became unexpectedly important during the time of the Covid-19 pandemic, but also go beyond the scope of this book in pertaining to new challenges such as AI tools and the learning environments they create. However, despite all the technological progress and development, global education will always have to deal with the diversity of learners – in many different aspects: culture, class, gender, language, migration, age, and numerous others. For all of them, it is important to use the learning outcomes presented here in the different contributions: how to understand diversity, how to work together, and how to learn in collaborative settings. As editors, we hope to contribute our share to the field by publishing this volume, which presents so many and such deep experiences and reflections.

Finally, we would like to say a heartfelt »thank you« to all the authors who did their best to present their expertise, deal with so many challenges of time, workload, and much more, and make it possible for us to compile this inspiring volume. We would also like to extend our deepest thanks to Hilal Sahin, the student assistant who worked hard on the manuscripts, and to the publisher who made it possible to present the rich fruits of our collaboration in this form.

May every reader experience at least as much joy and inspiration from the book as we had while working on it.

Anselm Böhmer
Götz Schwab
Illie Isso

References

Anthonysamy, L., Choo, K. A., & Hin, H. S. (2021). Investigating self-regulated learning strategies for digital learning relevancy. *Malaysian Journal of Learning and Instruction, 18*(1), 29–64.

Böhmer, A., Isso, I., Schwab, G., Sahin, H. (2022). Blended Learning Mobility – Konzepte, Erfahrungen, Perspektiven aus dem Projekt »Digital and International Virtual Academic Cooperation« (DIVA). *Ludwigsburger Beiträge zur Medienpädagogik*, Ausgabe 22/2022. URL: https://www.medienpaed-ludwigsburg.de/article/view/429

Petronzi, R. & Petronzi, D. (2020). The Online and Campus (OaC) model as a sustainable blended approach to teaching and learning in higher education: A response to COVID-19. *Journal of Pedagogical Research, 4*(4), 498–507.

Schwab, G., Oesterle, M., Whelan, A. (Eds.) (2022). *Promoting Professionalism, Innovation and Transnational Collaboration. A new approach to foreign language teacher education*. Research Publishing Net.

Waldman, T., Harel, E., & Schwab, G. (2019). Extended telecollaboration practice in teacher education: Towards pluricultural and plurilingual proficiency. *European Journal of Language Policy*, 11(2), 167–185.

Theoretical Approaches

Working on Concepts as an Element of Communication and Starting Point for research-based Learning in Higher Education

Viktoria Rieber, Anja Vocilka, Stine Albers, Sarah Gaubitz, & Bettina Blanck

1. Output and overview

Conceptual clarification work as an examination of things – whether these are accessible extraspectively or introspectively – and which aims at understanding and grasping their nature, is constitutive for being human. Even babies actively open up their world and find their way in it by groping, comparing, trying out, identifying and also thinking further (for example, in counterfactual thinking from about 18 months) and relating to it and other people (Gopnik, 2009). Conceptual work, in this sense, is a process that starts with the respective subjects and is shaped by the respective individual and historical-cultural life situations. Conceptual work becomes a social negotiation process when it comes to cooperative coexistence and mutual understanding. Language plays an important role in this process because it makes it possible to summarize concepts with one or a few words. At this point, various challenges can arise, as will be explained in the second section of the paper. How can we deal with these challenges in educational courses without overwhelming students? Our thesis is, that the starting point for such didactic ideas should be the individual (subjective) views of the world. From this vantage point, a view of manifold other worlds of understanding can be opened up, and intersubjective worlds of understanding can be created (Section 3). What this can look like and what concrete challenges it can mean for students and lecturers will then be discussed using the example of a seminar design for students of the elementary school subject »Sachunterricht«[1]. Through digitization, opportunities and limitations of cross-university and multilingual seminar designs are shown (Section 4).

The article concludes with a summary of some basic theses on the relevance of conceptual work as an educational responsibility, and with the concept of clarification-promoting conceptual work for science, education, and democratization advocated here (Section 5).

2. Locating in the diversity of different understandings of »concept« and on the relevance of conceptual work

There are extensive discussions about what was and is understood by a »concept« and how relations between individual and socially shared concepts, their respective objects/things/referents and their designations/words/terms are to be thought of. These discussions include the question of whether to distinguish between individual and socially shared terms at all – as is done in this text – or not. For insight into the diversity of different understandings, see, for example, the articles on the keyword »concept« in the Philosophical Dictionary of Philosophy (Ritter 1971) and the keynote article on »concept« by Eric Margolis and Stephen Laurence in the Stanford Encyclopedia of Philosophy (2019). Barbara C. Malt et al., following a series of quotations on different understandings of »concept«, state: »It is an unsatisfactory situation when researchers believe that something is fundamental to mental life, but they cannot articulate exactly what that something is« (2015, 314).

Sue Ellen Wright (2003) describes how problems with the different understandings of the term »concept« are potentiated by multilingualism. We cannot address this diversity of positions and the fundamental philosophical issues related to them, such as the idealism-realism problem, within the scope of this article. It is fundamental to our understanding of the term »concept« that we start from the thinking subject and not, for example, from a human-independent »platonic« conceptual world. In this respect, our understanding can be called »constructivist«. In this view, conceptual understanding does not have to be language based, even though language is a particularly socially relevant learning medium. We thus distance ourselves from positions that equate

---

1   »Sachunterricht« is an elementary school subject in Germany that includes »science« and »social studies«.

thinking with speaking, as well as from those that hold that language has nothing to do with thinking (for more details on this spectrum of different views on the relation between thinking and speaking, see Dörner, 2006).

Medin et al. describe the close connection between concept, language and culture: »Concepts matter, and [...] so does the language we use to describe them and the cultural practices in which we embed them« (2015, 349). They substantiate this thesis by reference to the example of biological category formation related to »Humans, Nonhuman Animals, Plants, and the Hierarchical Relations among Living Things« (2015, 350). In comparative cultural studies, they show, for example, that the understanding of »animal« as a possible generic term for humans may or may not vary depending on the respective culture. In the first case, there is an understanding of »Animal« as Animal-inclusive and in the second case, as Animal-contrastive. If both meanings reflect valid usage in a particular society, such as in Western English-speaking countries, the word is regarded as »polysemous«. By contrast, for example, the Indonesian word for »Animal« is understood only as Animal-contrastive (Medin et al., 2015).

In other studies – to give another example – European American and Menominee children and adults (fishermen) in Wisconsin are compared with each other concerning their respective conceptual ideas about nature. And although »groups had comparable knowledge bases, including ecological knowledge, there were substantial differences in how the knowledge was organized. European American experts favoured a taxonomic organization, and Menominee experts an ecological organization« (2015, 369). This difference was also found among children (ibid.). Cultural orientations can also be found among the scientists themselves: »While indigenous sciences focus on interspecies relations and mutual dependency – supporting perceptions of cooperation and socialization among nonhuman species – Western sciences have a tradition of focusing on individual species and fitness – assuming competition among species« (2015, 370).

As far as education is concerned, we further emphasize in our understanding of *concept* the idea of subjectivity developing in an intersubjectivity-enabling direction. In doing so, we are concerned with the critical-reflective involvement of subjects (Albers & Blanck, 2022) as a process of expanding and changing their previous understandings, whereby the end of the path is not predetermined (Albers & Blanck, 2021). What matters most is scientific and intersubjective involvement.

We distinguish (following the principle of the Semiotic Triangle, as propounded, for example, by Ogden and Richards (1923)) between concepts as mental representations (meanings/concepts) that refer to abstract or concrete things (objects), and words (expressions/terms) that can be used to refer to what has been conceptualized. Even though, as Wright (2003) explains, there are now more complex modes of representation than the semiotic triangle, the latter still represents the fundamental relationship between concept, word, and object. Since misunderstandings due to translations have repeatedly occurred here (Wright, 2003), we use both English and German terms in the representation of the Semiotic Triangle, the terms being often assigned to the corners in this way:

Illustration 1: Semiotic Triangle

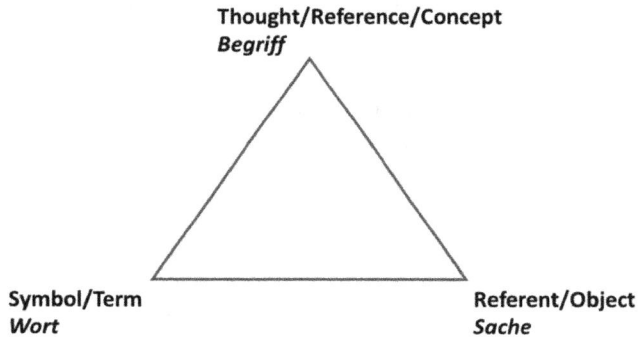

Thought/Reference/Concept
Begriff

Symbol/Term   **Referent/Object**
Wort   *Sache*

(inspired by Odgen & Richards (1923))

A well-known example can illustrate the complicated relationship between words, concepts, and objects from literature (e.g., Wright, 2003). The planet Venus (object) was initially comprehended in two different ways: in conceptual understanding 1, by which it was linguistically referred to as the »morning star« (word), and through conceptual understanding 2, whereby it was expressed linguistically as the »evening star«. One possessed two terms and two abstract concepts, each referring to the one object (seen from later knowledge) conceptually, so that it was constructed as two objects. Only with understanding 3, called »Venus«, could the other two conceptualizations be identified as two ways of construing the same object that could be reconciled with one another. This example is particularly interesting because it involves mutually compatible perspectives rather than mutually exclusive ones.[2] Moreover, the terms offer us further mutually exclusive meanings. Thus, we also use »morning star« to refer to a medieval striking weapon and »Venus« to refer to the Roman goddess of love. A horizon of possible misunderstandings, which would have to be comprehensively elaborated further, may be indicated by the following three questions: Do we look at an object/issue from different or common perspectives? Are the understandings represented compatible or incompatible? Does one use equal or unequal terms to denote the respective understanding? On the basis of combinatorial logic alone, these three questions yield eight possible sources of misunderstanding. A knowledge of this scope of potential misunderstandings is especially relevant for communication between people with dissimilar life-world references.

Central to the idea of conceptual work presented here is the principle of taking examples from the everyday world of the subjects as a starting-point. The subjective understandings described here are further developed in confrontations with alternative understandings. The goal is that as further understanding develops, the individual should find themselves presented with a spectrum of alternative understandings to be deliberated. This leads to a development of subjectivity in a direction conducive to intersubjectivity. The relationship between individual and socially shared conceptual understanding could be represented in the terms of the semiotic triangle as follows:

---

2   On the distinction between diversity as perspectivity and controversiality, especially alternativity, see Blanck Vocilka (i. pr.).

Illustration 2: The relationship between individual and socially shared conceptual understanding

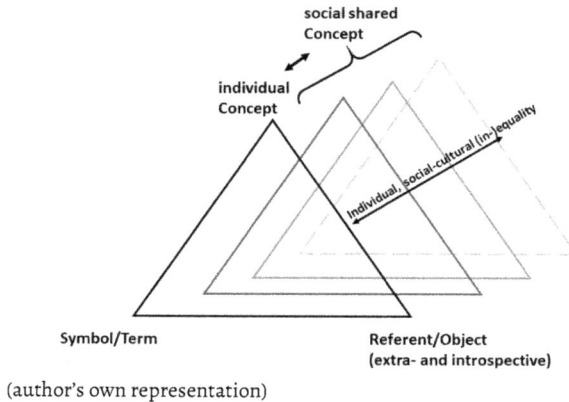

social shared
Concept

individual
Concept

Individual, social-cultural (in-)equality

Symbol/Term

Referent/Object
(extra- and introspective)

(author's own representation)

The knowledge of alternative understandings of the particular terms used is beneficial to clarification in several ways:

- Knowledge of alternative understandings opens up horizons of understanding for other people with their possibly different understandings. Examples are helpful here, as they can clarify understanding across different life worlds (including different languages). Suppose the following case: Someone explains their understanding of an object/issue using a variety of examples and citing alternative understandings, for deliberation. This provides a far broader basis for others to contribute their respective understandings and to enter into a joint clarification process than if someone presents a single understanding alone. Such conceptual work can also be described as »deliberation-oriented«.[3]

---

3   For the concept of a deliberation orientation, see e.g. Blanck 2004 or 2021. In the concept of a deliberation orientation, the alternatives considered appropriate to a particular problem are regarded as deliberate validity conditions for assessing the quality of a solution. Considered alternatives are to be preserved in this function as a deliberate validity condition. Transferred to conceptual explanations and conceptual clarification work, this means being able to use the knowledge of alternative understandings to advertise one's own understanding, as well as to be able to identify and comprehend other understandings. Given a critically reflective knowledge of non-knowledge, deliberation orientation assumes that further improvements of deliberations are possible which may lead to changes in the respective conceptualizations. Uncritical

- If this knowledge of alternative understandings is accompanied by a critical-reflective awareness of its limitations, one maintains the awareness of further possible alternative understandings. In dealing with others, this can make one more cautious about not interpreting or overwhelming them with one's ideas projectively. Also, this reflective knowledge increases one's willingness to correct one's understanding, if necessary, when there are further alternative interpretations appropriate to the given situation. Conversely, a basic knowledge of possible alternative constructions is a good step towards preventing oneself being overwhelmed by others' conceptual worlds. Asking for alternative understandings to be considered and deliberated upon creates an emancipatory potential that can protect subjectivity from being overwhelmed.
- This kind of conceptual work also opens up a critical and reflective approach to guidelines, e.g. scientific research on the subject matter. Even if it makes sense to adopt proven conceptual explanations from others, the direct integration of subjectivity means, fundamentally, that these proven conceptual explanations must also allow themselves to be located within a horizon of possible understandings. This horizon is conceived from the beginning as a changeable one. In this respect, such conceptual work can also be described as »research-oriented« or »scientific«.

In the sense outlined above, it is inherent in conceptual work that it aims at intersubjective understanding and clarification. Thus such conceptual work also gains significance for a clarification-promoting approach to controversies and conflicts which are essential for developing living democracies. In this context, as indicated above, a critical-reflective knowledge of the possibilities of misunderstanding is particularly relevant. We see the furthering of deliberation-oriented conceptual clarification skills as an educational opportunity that – according to our thesis – can make a significant contribution to democratization.

---

overidentification with a particular understanding is replaced in a deliberation orientation through an identity of engagement without losing the ability of critical distancing (Blanck 2016), which is open for further developmental steps, including necessary corrections.

3. Conceptual work as an educational opportunity

As has already been explained, words are used differently depending on individual and socially shared understanding. The example of *work* will illustrate this.

Work seems to be focused on and socially present as gainful employment. In Germany, for example, the state refers to unemployment as the condition of a person not being gainfully employed (Sozialgesetzbuch (Social Security Code; SGB) III §16 (1)). Especially from an educational point of view (e.g. in science and social studies) a modern concept of *work* should also include care work such as housework, family work and volunteer work (see Rieber, Queisser & Häußler, 2023 and Gläser, 2004). However, a research study on the professional knowledge of elementary school teachers regarding the meaning of the term »gainful employment« (Albers, 2014) showed that elementary school teachers might also have an understanding of *work* as gainful employment. In the study, two teachers stated that children whose parents were affected by unemployment were unaware of the advantages of work or had a negative attitude towards it (ibid.). It is then also problematic that prejudices are voiced against the unemployed and their children.

The individual use of a word seems to be important in conceptual work with prospective teachers (Albers, 2019). In addition to a scientific examination of the term »concept« and the work on selected concepts (see Section 2), as well as an educational examination of conceptual work with regard to school practice (see Section 4), it can also be about person-related work (Albers, 2014). This then means promoting the development of subjectivity in the students during the conceptual clarification work, which can also be understood as a critical-reflective examination of one's own understanding of concepts as an *educational opportunity*.

How far we can speak here of *educational* processes is a question answered in quite different ways in educational theory.[4] The English term »education« can be translated into German as both »Erziehung« and »Bildung«. Those two different terms are accompanied by overlapping concepts which leads to intensive discussions in the German-speaking part of the world. *Bildung* goes beyond the acquisition or development of specific competencies – which would

---

4   In the following, we refer to the description of a »transformational education« according to Hans-Christoph Koller, who further developed the concept of Rainer Kokemohr (see Koller, 2018, for more details).

rather correspond to *Erziehung*. *Bildung* means the reflective interaction of self and world (Humboldt 1960–81, Volume I, 64). The trigger for an educational process understood in this way is a moment of perceived intrapersonal irritation (Koller, 2018). According to Koller, such irritation can be described as an experience of »foreignness«. For a more precise definition of such experiences, he invokes Bernhard Waldenfels' concept of »the alien«. This »alien« is not only unknown to us (i.e. not only »the other«), but also calls ourselves into question (Waldenfels, 1997 and 2011).

In terms of conceptual work as an educational process, this means directing attention to moments of irritation and one's experiences of foreignness instigated by them, opening up to them and enduring them. Transcultural concepts could stimulate particular individual ways of dealing with one's alienness.

4. Conceptual work as a constitutive element of the educational methodology of Sachunterricht in higher education

The elementary school teacher qualification in Germany consists of a bachelor's and master's degree program as well as a practical phase, which is part of the qualification process and usually lasts 18 months. *Sachunterricht* is the third core subject in elementary school, along with Mathematics and German, and is accordingly chosen as a teaching subject by many students in teacher-training.

4.1 Presentation of our seminar conception

The importance of conceptual clarification work with prospective teachers has already been pointed out in the previous section using the example of the concept of work, which is understood in its simplest form as gainful employment. At this point, our seminar conception, which understands conceptual work as a constitutive element of teaching *Sachunterricht* in university and elementary school, will be explained in more detail.[5] Conceptual work is a process of in-depth questioning and researching that students must first discover and develop for themselves. If students and future teachers deal with the respective content in a conceptually clarifying way and prepare topics accordingly, a

---

5   The conception of the seminar with reference to the teaching methodology of »Sachunterricht« was also presented in Rieber & Vocilka (i. pr.).

motivating questioning and researching teaching can be initiated, e.g. using philosophical conversations. This assumption is the basis of our seminar conception. The seminar conception itself consists of two parts. The students' scientific examination of a socially relevant concept takes place in the first part. The second part deals with the educational challenge of transferring central conceptual aspects into a short story sequence as a starting point for philosophical conversations with primary school children. The seminar is aimed at students of elementary education in the master's program at the Ludwigsburg University of Education. It is designed as a bi-weekly four-hour seminar with a workload of four ECTSP, corresponding to 120 hours.

After an understanding of the various versions of concepts and an examination of the relevance of conceptual clarification work as already described (Section 2), the students apply what they have learned by dealing with a selected socially relevant concept. Throughout the first part of the seminar, and thus also in the first sessions and the periods in between, these discussions are focused on. For this purpose, fixed small groups, each consisting of three students, are formed to deal with a socially relevant term chosen by them for the entire semester, taking a multidisciplinary approach after formulating their initial core ideas based on literature. They identify and shape structures in the concepts, can narrow them down or expand them, discover and sustain controversies, and develop core ideas, core questions, and core statements. They search for their positionings and can justify or question them. Half-hour poster presentations by the respective groups in the seminar context serve as both seminar conclusion and (partial) examination performance. The students' work focuses on the step-by-step development of core statements that describe the socially relevant concept selected by the respective small groups. This developmental work takes place over the course of the seminar in a three-step process of core questions, core ideas, and core statements. First, the student groups pose core questions about their concept. This helps to clarify the concept by being formulated in an open-ended way. Core ideas are less well-honed and thought-out precursors of core statements and drafts of core statements. Core statements describe a particular concept in a concise, pointed, and summarizing manner.

Several core statements are required to describe and explain a concept. The individual statements can focus on essential sub-aspects; only the sum of all core statements comprehensively describes the concept to be clarified. The literature-based discussion of the concept goes into the core statements. Also, (scientific, intra- and interdisciplinary) controversies and ambivalences should be reflected in the core statements or the explanations. The core statements are then presented in the agreed form and phrasing on the poster as the currently valid finding.

Following this scientific clarification of concepts in a teaching seminar, (future) teachers are intended to meet the challenge of guiding conceptual work in elementary school. According to Köhnlein, conceptual work appears as a complex, socially guided process of composition, discrimination, structuring, and abstraction, which often only succeeds in a continuing series of approximations (Köhnlein, 2012). What lends itself well to this purpose is joint reflection in the context of philosophical discussion intended to be stimulated by a story about the concept to be clarified. Stories are what Köhnlein calls crystallization points for the initiation of concept work. This kind of joint story-based philosophizing can also be a way for students to expand or change their thinking (e.g. Michalik, 2018). Thus, writing a story sequence that challenges students to think about and engage with the concept thematicized in the story forms the centerpiece of the second part of the seminar. This story is presented in writing by the seminar participants, together with the associated objectives and incorporated core statements, and defended in a colloquium. The development of a story as a starting point for example-based conceptual work in elementary school seems to us to be particularly suitable since examples, as we have already presented them as an educational approach to conceptual clarification, can be integrated into the writing of a story developed into one. By creating a context, a story provides emotional access to the core of the concept. This can enable school-age readers to personally identify with the thematic issues, especially if there are protagonists in the story who are the same age as elementary students and move in their life worlds. At the same time, the story also makes it possible to distance oneself from the protagonists. Distancing and objectification are essential so that the content does not overwhelm and intimidate the students. Both identification and distancing can make stories a motivating approach to conceptual work. The fact that stories are able to illustrate abstract concepts through concreteness can also contribute to this. This leads to a materialization of the symbolic, so to speak. Stories can contribute to low-threshold access to the discussion of concepts through references to the world of life, and in doing so provide learning occasions through irritation or conflict concerning *familiar* things. In this way »zones of proximal development« (following Vygotsky 1987) are opened up to students. Examples of criteria for a story providing opportunities for philosophical deliberation of a concept are, in our view, the following: A (philosophical) story should make the content of core statements previously developed available for an addressee-oriented discussion; the story should provoke readers into asking *real* (in the sense of meaningful) questions, should open wider horizons of thought, and should offer different ways of thinking about the concept relevant to the story. Students should be stimulated into engaging with problematic or conflicting elements of the story without having recourse to stigmatizations, stereotypes, and clichés.

This seminar was designed and conducted in the summer semester of 2019 as an attendance-only seminar. Due to the corona pandemic, the seminar was then held as an online class for four semesters starting in the summer semester of 2020, testing and using both asynchronous and synchronous formats. For our seminar, too, »the pandemic acted as a catalyst for a transformation process« (Schultz-Pernice et al., 2021, 36). Thus, in the summer semester of 2022, the further developed seminar contained both face-to-face and synchronous online sessions, with the face-to-face meetings comprising approximately 60% of the seminar time. In the face-to-face sessions at the university, the focus was on joint content discussion and in-depth work in the individual concept groups. The now scarcer face-to-face time was used more specifically for teaching competencies and attitudes in areas where face-to-face teaching has its strengths, such as developing new research questions or promoting professional identity development (Schultz-Pernice et al., 2021). The online format was used mainly for exchange across groups. With about 90 participating students, we could easily and quickly open numerous virtual sub-spaces within the main virtual seminar space, where a few concept groups presented their posters and engaged in a critical-constructive exchange about them. At the same time, split screens allowed an equally good view of the presented poster content. Feedback to the group was not only possible orally, but also in writing via chat. The same applied to the stories developed; here, the virtual space offered flexible possibilities that university facilities could not provide in a comparable form, especially for large groups of students. Digital options support students and can lead to the relief of problems caused by large-group physical presence. For example, students first record example-based discussions of their conceptual groups in audio recordings, post a sequence of about fifteen minutes from these discussions in the digital seminar course and invite the other participants to think about and discuss them. This type of asynchronous discussion in online forums is explained in more detail in the following section.

4.2 Opportunities and challenges of a cross-university and multilingual digital seminar design

Digitization opens up opportunities to apply the seminar concept described in section 4.1 to multilingual teams of students and university lecturers who are dispersed over a wide geographical area. Such a conception can make (extended) transformative educational processes possible, as students from different locations, even across national borders, can bring a large and varied spectrum of experience to bear on the seminar, together with more widely ranging critical perspectives and additional issues. In this collaboration and reflection, meanings of concepts can be constructed, explored, resolved, and affirmed. Such a cross-locational seminar is made possible by various synchronous and asynchronous online teaching and learning settings, which will be explored below in relation to conceptual work.

With regard to more in-depth conceptual work, it should be noted that in cross-university or cross-locational collaboration, even more perspectives and concepts can be included, or knowledge from more diverse sources can be drawn upon for the multidisciplinary discussions, as, for example, Chen and Sun (2016) also point out. Particularly challenging but also fruitful can be the comparison on a meta-level focusing on different languages (cf. Section 2)

The asynchronous digital formats, particularly, can be conducive to intensive conceptual work. Individuals can work intensively on the terms in asynchronous discussions or reflect on whether the texts are factually concise enough. Individuals can read the respective contributions repeatedly, refer back to them again and again, and post their individual ideas at their own pace: »In addition, because individuals have to explicitly express their thoughts in writing, the very process of writing in itself helps them to carefully construct their ideas (Vonderwell, 2003), as well as encourages reflection which helps promote higher level learning such as analysis, synthesis, and evaluation (Newman et al. 1997)« (Hew, Cheung & Ng, 2010, 572).

At the same time, texts written in asynchronous online forums, for example, retain a certain dialogic character and are more personal and informal than other forms of academic writing. Thus, a kind of community of practice can be established among the participating students and faculty, who strive for a precise type of dialogic communication that stimulates or presupposes reflection. Ideas can be critically analyzed and complex meanings negotiated to establish a culture of reflection. As a result, students are naturally guided toward a systematic construction of meaning that involves planning, structuring, and fa-cilitating discourse toward a clear goal, such as a poster (cf. Section 4.1)

Furthermore, an advantage of such online teaching-learning settings is that, in addition to the better opportunities for accessing and collaborating with people around the world, participation can be higher, as even less ac-cessible target-audience groups, such as shy people and minorities, can be reached and are likely to get more involved in online settings than in face-to-face classes, as pointed out by e.g., Lamnek & Krell (2016) and Sun & Chen (2016). This is particularly significant for cross-university and cross-locational seminars. Moreover, students perceive online discussions as fairer and more democratic than discussions in a physical seminar setting (Fernandez Polo & Varela, 2017). However, online discussions are perceived by students in asynchronous settings as less collaborative and more individualistic, and the sense of belonging also decreases compared with that in synchronous online discussions. Students rate these as more focused, more motivating, and with a stronger sense of belonging within the group (Fabriz, 2021). The sense of belonging in online learning and teaching settings should be given special attention, as numerous studies have shown a strong correlation between social interaction, a sense of community, and their role in success in online learning (Sun & Chen, 2016; Fabriz, 2021). Especially in cross-locational or cross-university settings, the social context poses a significant challenge be-cause students do not know each other, and language or other barriers can make social interaction additionally difficult. Several measures are available to help deal with these challenges. For example, blended learning formats in which students can first get to know each other on-site prove to be very helpful (Zahn, Rack & Paneth, 2021), but promoting individual responsibilities and formulating group goals (Johnson & Johnson, 1994) are also highly conducive practical measures.

5. Conceptual work as an educational task

As the preceding explanations have made clear, the conceptual work proposed here focuses on a deliberation-oriented unfolding of subjectivity which is nei-ther overridden by objectivity, nor conceived of as its replacement. Instead, this emphasis on subjectivity aims to open up possible alternative understandings of terms to be clarified in each case, so that individuals can further develop and locate themselves with their understandings and knowledge within a horizon of possible alternative interpretations. In this way a development of subjectivity towards intersubjectivity takes place. This is achieved by embedding one's understanding in the knowledge of alternative understandings. This process is accompanied by a critical-reflective awareness of the limitations of the ability to grasp alternative understandings and a critical-reflective knowledge of non-knowledge, which promotes a research (scientific) attitude. There is an openness to other understandings, which can also lead to possible distancing from one's previous understanding. The prior understanding does not thereby become worthless. It now belongs to the horizon of possible interpretations and is part of the context of justification for the new understanding. Furthermore, it can continue to inform processes of opinion and viewpoint formation and contribute to techniques of reasoning and argument.

Alternative-conscious conceptual work goes hand in hand with an emancipatory potential for the individual and enlightenment or clarification possibilities when dealing with controversies,

especially alternatives. In our view, this makes conceptual work conceived in this way an educational and research desideratum. Education, research orientation/science and democratization are brought into a mutually reinforcing context in a special way. For student teachers, no matter what type of school they are training for or subjects they are studying, this potential seems to us to be particularly relevant. As part of their educational mission, they can promote science and democratization from the very beginning in their future professional field through appropriate conceptual.

References

Albers, S. (2019). Ein Plädoyer für personenbezogene Arbeit im Hochschulstudium. In: J. Studer, E. Abplanalp, & S. Disler, (Eds.), *Persönlichkeitsentwicklung in Hochschulausbildungen fördern. Aktuelles aus Forschung und Praxis* (pp. 11–22). hep verlag.

Albers, S. (2014). *Das Thema »Erwerbslosigkeit« in der Lehrer-/-innenbildung für den Sachunterricht an der Grundschule*. Baltmannsweiler: Schneider Verlag Hohengehren (Sachunterrichtsdidaktik und Grundschulpädagogik. Beiträge zu Forschung und Entwicklung, 1).

Albers, S. & Blanck, B. (2021). Herausforderungen von Optimierungen als Dekontextualisierungen. In: *Pädagogische Rundschau*, 75(6), 695–702.

Albers, S. & Blanck, B. (2022). Kritische Reflexivität als Ausgang für Entfaltung von Subjektivität im Grundschullehramtsstudium. In: E. Gläser, J. Poschmann, P. Büker, & S. Miller (Eds.), *Reflexion und Reflexivität im Kontext Grundschule: Perspektiven für Forschung, Lehrer:innenbildung und Praxis* (pp. 295–300). Klinkhardt.

Blanck, B. (2004). Erwägungsorientierung. In: *Information Philosophie 32*(1), 42–47.

Blanck, B. (2016). Distanzfähiges Engagement: Mit Vielfalt und Unübersichtlichkeit erwägungsorientiert-deliberativ umgehen. In: *IDE-Online Journal* (International Dialogues on Education: Past and Present). *3*(3), no pages.

Blanck, B. (2021). Erwägungsorientierter Umgang mit kontroversen Alternativen und reflexivem Wissen um Nicht-Wissen als Chance für Demokratisierung durch vielperspektivischen Sachunterricht. In: T. Simon (Ed.), *Demokratie im Sachunterricht – Sachunterricht in der Demokratie* (pp. 105–115). Springer.

Blanck, B. & Vocilka, A. (2023). Diversität als Perspektivität *und* Kontroversität beim Philosophieren mit Schüler*innen am Beispiel »Weihnachtszeit«. In: S. May-Krämer, K. Michalik, & A. Nießeler (Eds.), *Philosophieren im Sachunterricht – Potentiale und Perspektiven für Forschung, Lehre und Unterricht*. Bad Heilbrunn: Klinkhardt.

Dörner, Dietrich (2006). Sprache und Denken. In: J. Funke (Ed.), *Denken und Problemlösen. Enzyklopädie der Psychologie*, Topic C, Series II Volume 8 (pp. 619–646). Hogrefe.

Fabriz, S., Mendzheritskaya, J., & Stehle, S. (2021). Impact of Synchronous and Asynchronous Settings of Online Teaching and Learning in Higher Education on Students' Learning Experience During COVID-19. *Frontiers in Psychology*, 12:733554. doi : 10.3389/fpsyg.2021.733554.

Fernandez Polo, F.J. & Varela, M.C. (2017). A Description of Asynchronous Online Discussions in Higher Education: In: *EPiC Series in Language and Linguistics*, 2, 256–264.

Gläser, E. (2004). Soziale Ungleichheit: Arbeitslosigkeit. In: A. Kaiser & D. Pech (Eds.), *Die Welt als Ausgangspunkt des Sachunterrichts* (pp. 132–136). Schneider Verlag Hohengehren (Basiswissen Sachunterricht, 6).

Gopnik, Alison (2009). *The Philosophical Baby: What Children's Minds Tell Us About Truth, Love, and the Meaning of Life*. Random House.

Hew, K.F., Cheung, W.S., & Ng, C.S.L. (2010). Student contribution in asynchronous online discussion: a review of the research andempirical exploration. In: *Instructional Science*, 38(6), 571–606.

Humboldt, W. v. (1960–1981). *Werke in fünf Bänden*, ed. by A. Flitner & K. Giel. Wissenschaftliche Buchgesellschaft.

Johnson, D. W. & Johnson, R.T. (1994). *Learning Together and Alone. Cooperative, Competitive, and Individualistic Learning* (Fourth Edition). Interaction Book Company

Köhnlein, W. (2012). *Sachunterricht und Bildung*. Klinkhardt.

Kokemohr, R. (2007). Bildung als Welt- und Selbstentwurf im Fremden. Annäherungen an eine Bildungsprozesstheorie. In: H.-C. Koller, W. Marotzki, & O. Sanders (Eds.), *Bildungsprozesse und Fremdheitsbestimmung. Beiträge zu einer Theorie transformatorischer Bildungsprozesse* (pp. 13–68). transcript.

Koller, H.-C. (2018). *Bildung anders denken. Einführung in die Theorie transformatorischer Bildungsprozesse*. Kohlhammer.

Lamnek, S. & Krell, C. (2016). *Qualitative Sozialforschung*. 6., vollständig überarbeitete Auflage. Beltz.

Malt, B. C., Gennari, S. P., Imai, M., Ameel, E., Saji, N., & Majid, A. (2015). Where Are the Concepts? What Words Can and Can't Reveal. In: E. Margolis & S. Laurence (Eds.), *The Conceptual Mind* (pp. 291–326). The MIT Press.

Margolis, E. & Laurence, S. (2019). »Concepts«. In: *The Stanford Encyclopedia of Philosophy* (Summer 2019 Edition), edited by E. Zalta. Url: https://plato.stanford.edu/entries/concepts/ (10.07.22).

Medin, D., Ojalehto, B., Waxmann, S. & Bang, M. (2015). Relations: Language, Epistemologies, Categories, and Concepts. In: E. Margolis & S. Laurence (Eds.), *The Conceptual Mind* (pp. 349–378). The MIT Press.

Michalik, K. (2018). Ungewissheit als Herausforderung und Chance – Perspektiven von Lehrerinnen und Kindern auf das philosophische Gespräch. In: H. De Boer & K. Michalik (Eds.), *Philosophieren mit Kindern. Forschungszugänge und -perspektiven* (pp. 175–187). Barbara Budrich.

Odgen, C. K. & Richards, I. A. (1923). *The Meaning of Meaning. A Study of the Influence of Language upon Thought and of the Science of Symbolism*. Harcourt, Brace & World.

Rieber, V. & Vocilka, A. (2023). »Begriffe sind das Papiergeld des Denkens«. Begriffsarbeit als konstitutives Element des Sachunterrichts in Hochschule und Grundschule. In: S. May-Krämer, K. Michalik, & A. Nießeler (Eds.), *Philosophieren im Sachunterricht – Potentiale und Perspektiven für Forschung, Lehre und Unterricht* (pp. 71-81). Klinkhardt.

Rieber, V., Queisser, U. & Häußler, A. (2023): Care-Arbeit. Blinder Fleck mit didaktischem Potenzial, HiBiFo – Haushalt in Bildung & Forschung, 2–2023 (pp. 40–53). https://doi.org/10.3224/hibifo.v12i2.04

Ritter, J. (Ed.) (1971). *Historisches Wörterbuch der Philosophie*. Volume 1: A-C. Wissenschaftliche Buchgesellschaft.

Schultz-Pernice, F., Becker, S., Berger, S., Ploch, N., Radkowitsch, A., Vejvoda, J., & Fischer, F. (2021). Digitales Lehren und Lernen an der Hochschule: Erkenntnisse aus der empirischen Lehr-Lernforschung. Teil 1: Planung und Gestaltung digitaler Lehre. *Lehrerbildung@LMU, 1*(2). 35–51.

Sun, A. & Chen, X. (2016). Online education and its effective practice: A research review. Journal of Information Technology Education: Research, *15*, 157–190.

Vygotskij, L. S. (1987). Thinking and speech. In: R.W. Rieber & A. S. Carton (Eds.), *The collected Works of L. S. Vygotsky*, Volume 1: Problems of general psychology. Plenum.

Waldenfels, Bernhard (2011). *Phenomenology of the alien: basic concepts*. Transl. from the German by Alexander Kozin and Tanja Stähler. Northwestern Univ. Press.

Waldenfels, Bernhard (1997). *Topografie des Fremden. Studien zur Phänomenologie des Fremden*. Fischer.

Wright, S. E. (2003). From the Semiotic Triangle to the Semantic Web. In: *Terminology Science & Research. Journal of the International Institute for Terminology Reasearch* (IITF), *14*, 111–135.

Zahn, C., Rack, O. & Paneth, L. (2021). Grundbausteine engagierter Zusammenarbeit in Lerngruppen. In: O. Geramanis, S. Hutmacher, & L. Walser (Eds.), *Kooperation in der digitalen Arbeitswelt. Verlässliche Führung in Zeiten virtueller Kommunikation* (pp. 161–174). Springer.

Problematising »Cultural Competence« in the Digital Environment

Jon Mason, Karen Cieri, & Chris Spurr

1. Introduction

Terminology can be a challenge, whether in public or academic discourse. It can test political correctness, be opaque as an academic construct, or become embedded as some cute new morphing meme. Creative »turns of phrase« emerge daily, often with roots in popular culture and the hyper-networked worlds of social media. But just as such expressions might enrichen culture, they can also hinder effective communication. At the interface of intercultural understanding, choice of terminology can be particularly problematic. Terms can be – and routinely are – appropriated because they suddenly appear within social discourse, seem useful and then get used within diverse contexts beyond their origins. Because of this, concepts and their associated terms and definitions are not always semantically aligned within a language, let alone in translation. And so, it is not so difficult to make a linguistic faux pas in cross-cultural communication. This chapter focuses on this terminology problem in presenting a review of »cultural competence« in the research literature, particularly that literature associated with intercultural understanding. This term is problematised because it can imply elitist perspectives or be interpreted too narrowly. To sharpen the focus, this problematic is situated within the context of the evolving digital environment – the medium through which teaching and learning in the twenty first century is increasingly utilised.

2. Terminology and Public Discourse

Terminology can be the source of protracted debate and a problem that is more than just »academic«. For example, prominent in the era of »post-truth« has been public criticism of news media reporting with widespread usage of terms such as *fake news* by politicians to dismiss any news that they disagree with or contradicts their political messaging (Luo, Hancock, & Markowitz, 2022). Of course, prior to this situation the media has had a long history of sensationalising headlines to capture attention, so the politicians are not entirely to blame. Moreover, concentration of media ownership is a well-known source of political bias (Grossman, Margalit, & Mitts, 2022). The net result is mistrust of the media, making it difficult for the public to distinguish credible and unreliable sources of information (Cinelli, et al., 2021; Luo, Hancock, & Markowitz, 2022; Mari, et al., 2022). The contemporary context is further complicated by the proliferation of social media echo chambers where terms like »conspiracy theory« are used to denigrate or marginalize certain ideas or commentary, sidelining informed debate that is in the public interest (Cinelli, et al., 2021). Alongside these developments has been a broader decline in trust of public institutions and authorities, such as financial institutions, scientific agencies, churches, and governments (Lovari, 2020; Ognyanova, Lazer, Robertson, & Wilson, 2020). Consequently, public discourse in the contemporary global environment has become both polarized and tribalized, complicating the appreciation of both cultural difference and commonality (Congdon, 2022; Funkhouser, 2022). Thus, while the presence of terms like *global citizenship* in school curricula may signal development of intercultural skills as an essential »21st century skill«, the emerging reality suggests a trend toward »de-globalisation« and a retreat from the global perspectives (Schugurensky & Wolhuter, 2020; Williamson, 2021).

There are many more prominent examples of terminology adopted within public discourse that is »catchy« yet also ambiguous because of utility. The term »smart« is a good example. Since the arrival of the smartphone the idea of smart has been adopted in all kinds of contexts, describing the capabilities of the latest models of pens, fridges, cars, as well as »futureproofing« of urban design in smart cities (Daudkhane, 2017; Dron, 2018; Hoel & Mason, 2018; Pilon & Brouard, 2022). Recognising the pivotal role of terminology, international standards-setting organisations such as the International Organization for Standardization (ISO) routinely pay a lot of attention to it, whatever the domain of practice. For example, some terms such as *blockchain* or *big data* are relatively easy to define because they have technically precise semantic boundaries; others, such as *open* (as in open source, open access, open science, and open educational practices), have rich semantics and hence broad utility.

In the more select realms of academic discourse, concepts such as decolonization and cultural competence are often implicated within the broader public discourse of diversity, inclusion, and equity. While these terms are in widespread usage in academic contexts they are also contested (Arribas Lozano, 2018). Moreover, generalisations about people based on race is racist – »white educators mobilize and weaponize cultural competency discourses to justify blatant racism as well as protect themselves against allegations of the same this problem« (Ray & Davis, 2021). In the public domain, such terms are not easily adopted – arguably, because they can convey an elitist or in-crowd knowledge of the correct usage. The context of public policy discourse, intercultural development is often focused on things like peacebuilding, problem solving and conflict resolution. Within this broader context, then, choices are made concerning terminology alternatives.

In response to such terminology challenges, there has been a noticeable shift in policy relevant to the Australian education sector in recent years where a commitment to addressing systemic inequities is also evident. For example, the expression »cultural responsiveness« is now explicit within the Australian Northern Territory Government's *Education Strategy 2021–2025* and embedded within guidelines developed by the Australian Institute for Teaching and School Leadership (AITSL, 2022):

> The power of education to impact change cannot be overstated. For many, education is the means through which dreams and aspirations are realised. For others, though, education is something to be endured for little or no gain. The legacy of colonisation has undermined Aboriginal and Torres Strait Islander students' access to their cultures, identities, histories, and languages. Aboriginal and Torres Strait Islander students have not had access to a complete, relevant, and responsive education. Being an institution of the dominant or mainstream culture, Australian education systems reflect the values, norms and world views of that culture. Consequently, inequitable education outcomes have often been viewed as deficiencies or failures on the part of the student, rather than a failure of our systems. (AITSL, 2022)

The AITSL »Intercultural Development Continuum« begins with a recognition of »intercultural destructiveness« where »attitudes, policies and practices that are destructive to identities, values and practices«. Such recognition is not easily enacted and is complicated by the next stage described as »intercultural blindness ... the belief that all peoples have the same needs, priorities and values and that those who are different are segregated for their own good« (Australian Institute for Teaching and School Leadership, 2022). Moving on from these starting points enables pathways that extend through stages of intercultural awareness, competence, responsiveness and finally »intercultural sustainability«. In the practical context of teacher workshops focused on this, however, the nuancing is not universally appreciated nor is there easy consensus. With destructiveness and blindness explicit, coming to terms with such things can be emotional and shameful, linked to traumatic history. Arguably, workplace discussions around cultural development are often lacking in compassion. Anecdotally, improving intercultural skills can feel like either a compliance issue or treated as a simple matter of providing training around key concepts. Importantly, the intercultural interface is also about dialog, interpersonal relationships, self-awareness and personal growth. When confronted honestly and authentically, it can be tender transformation space with its subconscious shadows and sensitive tendrils needy of human connection.

3. Culture and Cultural Competence

Most literate people have a working understanding of what culture is and there are countless definitions that can be sourced defining it in terms of beliefs, values, attitudes, protocols, symbols, artefacts, or traditions associated with a particular group of people – and the relationship between religion and secular society also provides plenty of influence. Often, all these various aspects combine to invoke a sense of difference. But what may be acceptable within one culture may be perceived as oppressive in another – for example, the degree to which women's clothing may be considered revealing or not. At the intercultural interface it is easy to make a *faux pas* in ordinary daily activities such as making direct eye contact or signalling one is okay using a hand gesture. Importantly, culture is something that is learned, shared, and dynamic – it changes over time. In the field of intercultural studies several constructs can distinguish cultures according to the depth of »power distance« (hierarchy), individual versus collective values, degree of masculinity, »uncertainty avoidance«, perspectives on long-term conventions, and freedom versus restraint (Hofstede, 2001). While such classifications can be useful to consider they can also mask deeper complexity and perpetuate another problem – »othering«, amplifying difference over commonality (Canales, 2000; Reid, 2017). Social problems are also very much bound up in the »other«. The rise of conspiracy theories highlights this, particularly through the medium of social media. Moreover, can we really understand another culture through studying the conventions and protocols associated with it? Will training in the other group's protocols be sufficient for gaining »cultural competence«?

Like many words in English, »culture« has versatility and can be used meaningfully across a variety of contexts. For example, it may be used to refer to the visual and performing arts, the protocols for doing things within organisations, or the practices associated with a particular ethnic group (Balcazar, Suarez-Balcazar, & Taylor-Ritzler, 2009; Evans, et al., 2012). Where shared meaning is concerned, however, ambiguity often creeps in, and so additional qualification is used to provide clarity – as in »organisational culture« or »Chinese culture«. The flipside, however, is when the qualification brings ambiguity, and this notoriously happens in the context of intercultural communication. »Cultural competence« is a prime example and is prominent in »multicultural social work discourse« (Nadan, 2017). While sometimes used to describe proficiency in effectively communicating and interacting with people from different cultural backgrounds it is also commonly used to describe fundamental protocols and practices that an individual must learn about a specific cultural group. And, while the intention of gaining cultural competence may be to address underlying power imbalances and social inequalities, the term itself also can exacerbate the very »us and them« problem it aims to address because it implies the presence of insiders and outsiders. A deeper problem is that much of the framing around cultural competency of from a place of »whiteness« (Ray & Davis, 2021). But while it might make some sense to respectfully learn about the protocols for engagement with a remote First Nations community – and refer to that as the acquisition of cultural competence – it makes less sense in the converse, when suggesting someone might become a culturally competent Australian or a culturally competent Indonesian. Why does such a juxtaposition reveal conceptual dissonance? Some may argue it is because the one of the co-authors (Jon) who articulated the quandary has not questioned his own cultural position enough. But another argument is that flipping the context exposes the absurdity of the construct, and probably a false assumption cultural homogeneity in nation states.

»Cultural competence« also sits within a larger corpus of terminology aligned with inclusion and diversity that communicates politically correct overtones, although is also sometimes at odds with it (Chun & Evans, 2016, p. 8). Thus, similar expressions such as »cultural sensitivity« and »cultural humility« are sometimes used to describe an individual's ability to have awareness and respect for cultural differences (Botelho & Lima, 2020; Danso, 2018). The notion of humility is also inferred in the AITSL continuum where cultural responsiveness describes a poignant stage where people become vulnerable and are keenly aware of how hard these spaces can be. The resulting actions and relationships are then felt by all involved as authentic.

It is somewhat ironic, however, that »cultural competence« is still widely used when the academic literature focused on it has been debating its appropriateness for well over a decade (Botelho & Lima, 2020; Burgess, 2019; Chun & Evans, 2016; Kumagai & Lypson, 2009; Ray & Davis, 2021). It is not as if alternatives have not been proposed. Burgess (2019), for example, suggests that in the context of teacher professional development it would be preferable to focus more on »develop[ing] *critical reflexivity* in the ongoing construction of a pedagogical cultural identity«. For Chun and Evans (2016) the notion of »diversity competence« is preferable while for Kumagai and Lypson (2009) the foregrounding of »competence« in multicultural education blurs the more important role of »fostering critical awareness—a critical consciousness—of the self, others, and the world«. Why should competence matter at all? For us, the implied meaning is all about dialogic skills that are needed to negotiate the complexities of social interaction. If we embrace some »cultural humility« then we are opening our potentially wrong assumptions and views to others when we engage with them (Branson, 2020; Hockett, Samek & Headley, 2012; Reid, 2017).

At our university in the Northern Territory of Australia the context is explicitly remote and regional, and it is no surprise that there is a strong focus on partnering with First Nations people in our programs. In addition, a large international student cohort originating from over 60 countries provides an imperative for intercultural engagement. In recent years there has been a subtle shift to referring to »cultural competences« – that is, the plural form. This small change makes a significant difference because it infers diversity in the message more than ability.

4. Terminology and Technology Enhanced Learning

Likewise, in the fast-moving field of technology enhanced learning (TEL), there exists an expanding scope of terminology that is often adopted in very different ways and this can contribute to confusion within public discourse. The cluster of terms associated with »distance education« in the last three decades underscores this: *computer-based training, computer mediated communication, computer-supported collaborative learning, online learning, e-learning, digital learning, mobile learning*, and *technology enhanced learning* to name a few. A prominent contemporary example is the term »artificial intelligence« (AI). While this can refer to a branch of computer science that is approximately 70 years old, AI is now commonly used to describe entities such as robots (»an AI«) as well as a field of research and innovation (Mason, Peoples, & Lee, 2020). Arguably, AI also represents convenient shorthand for the widely adopted term »smart« (as in smart phones, smart cars, and smart cities) – the mainstream access to Chat-GPT during 2023 demonstrated very quickly that a new era of »smart technology« adoption using conversational agents is underway (Graesser & Forsyth, 2014; Li, Xing & Leite, 2022).

AI is also used in a broader sense to describe a wide range of technologies, from simple algorithms to advanced systems that can perform tasks that typically require human intelligence, such as natural language processing and image recognition. Not long ago, computer-based speech recognition was understood to be a sub-field of AI. But because AI is often used to describe such a wide range of technologies, the notion of the associated »intelligence« or capabilities is up for debate – just because a machine can compute does not necessarily make it »intelligent« (Verhulst, et al., 2021). Within the field of AI there are associated terms like »deep learning«, »machine learning«, and »computational intelligence« which are used to describe a diversity of algorithms and techniques, including what is also used within the field as »supervised« and »unsupervised« learning. As with any discipline, it takes time to gain familiarity with foundational categories and concepts.

Putting aside the academic debate as to whether «data is« or »data are« (arguably, both are now acceptable for people who appreciate the evolution of language), another example of confusing terminology is »big data«. Used to describe the large amounts of data generated by an expanding number of data points in our daily lives resulting from digital technologies supporting activities such as public transport usage or shopping in the supermarket (Cope & Kalantzis, 2015). Such data is routinely collected by both commercial organizations and individuals for analysis and monetization. However, the notion of »bigness« can be misleading because the datasets are not necessarily big in size but more typically in complexity or volume. In the broader domain of digital technology innovation terms such as »zero trust« have been coined to mean exactly the opposite to what most people would naturally assume – a robust layer of digital security that ensure trust!

When considering the specific TEL context of teacher education then we can also find an opportunity to connect the foregoing discussion on cultural humility to the evolving digital environment:

> A key goal of teacher education, therefore, is to prepare graduates to know that their job is predicated on a *lack* of knowledge, and that as digital global communications bring increasingly rapid cultural hybridity, cosmopolitanism and fallout from historical policy inequity, they will continually need to learn, over and over again, about their students' cultural and community ways of knowing, doing and thinking. (Reid, 2017, p. 210)

5. The Digital Environment

Depending on when the beginnings of the so-called digital revolution are conceived, various terms have been coined to describe the abilities and skills required to engage successfully with digital technology. Often, »literacy« is included as a qualifier as in *information literacy, computer literacy, ICT literacy, media literacy, digital literacy, data literacy*, etc. Literacy in this list could easily be replaced by »skills« to communicate much the same meaning. Related terminology also includes *computer expertise, digital fluency,* and *digital competence,* where knowledge, skills and attitudes might also be implied (Miller & Bartlett, 2012). In the context of lifelong learning in the 21st century there are several other considerations – for example, someone may be skilled at using social media but not be information literate or vice versa; someone may have developed excellent search skills but have no understanding of information provenance or cyber safety; or someone with physical disabilities may have developed extraordinary facility with a brain-computer interface for navigating the web but have no other digital technology skills. The popularised notion »digital natives« and »digital immigrants« have also perpetrated false generalisation of digital competence (Prensky, 2001). Many so-called digital natives have little knowledge or understanding of the digital environment beyond a narrow scope of smart-phone usage.

In a specific context of using digital technology for written academic argumentation, digital competence might refer to effective use of digital tools and resources to research, draft, revise, and publish written arguments (Arroyo, Fernández-Lancho & Martínez, 2021). But how is such competence conceived if the individual is also using AI text generators and paraphrasing tools? Such questions emerge if we are thinking critically. And we need to be asking more and more questions about our interactions *with and within* the digital environment. We have long passed that time when digital technology is accurately portrayed as »just a tool« (Gates, 1995; Zuboff, 2015). We are also immersed within an environment of digital culture, digital commerce, and digital learning within a growing context of the monetization of big data, surveillance, and the scaling up of cyber security threats worldwide.

6. Nuancing the Digital Divide

Prominent within the literature focused on engaging with digital technology is the notion of the »digital divide« (Coleman, 2021; Cruz-Jesus, Vicente, Bacao, & Oliveira, 2016). Basically, it refers to a disparity gap – between those who have access to digital technologies and those who do not. The concept emerged shortly after the invention of the world wide web though the underlying concept of social inequality dates back much further into history (Ragnedda & Muschert, 2015).

The COVID-19 pandemic has had a profound impact on the digital divide with significant consequences for education, healthcare, and daily life (Mason, Khan, & Badar, 2021; Norman, et al., 2022). Prior to the pandemic several global initiatives had promised solutions, often led by innovations with technology. The evidence is, however, that while this divide has widened significantly due to the pandemic, many technology-led solutions to the problem have not yet proved to be sustainable due to overlooking the importance of local contexts (Badar & Mason, 2020). Moreover, in responding to this problem and ensuring that all individuals have access to the opportunities provided by digital technologies other dimensions to the »divide« have emerged.

One of us has a role as a teacher in a remote a Northern Territory Indigenous community. Anecdotally, another form of digital divide is evident in such a setting where typically digital technology is used as a conduit for social capital and entertainment, as in the sharing photos and movies, more than a platform for information seeking or learning. The following is a rendering of a real-world dialog that took place in 2022 in a remote community within the Northern Territory of Australia…

It had been a busy day thus far dealing with students and making some phone calls to organise logistics for an upcoming event. At last, my office was quiet – here was a chance to get some uninterrupted time to plough through some report writing…. Or so I thought!

»Chris, Chris, are you there? Are you busy wawa (brother)?«

I hesitate, stare at my computer as it contemplates opening the excel spreadsheet file that I had clicked to open.

»I am yapa (sister), why?« I ask with a sigh, knowing full well that my yapa has brought her daughter to me once again to attempt to gain access to her MyGov account so we could complete her overdue tax returns from previous years.

»I've brought Phyllis so you can help her with her government djora (paperwork)« says my yapa.

Aaagghh I'm thinking, but already I find myself saying »Okay yapa, but we need to make it quick. I have other work to do and you really should make a time to come and …« My words trail off.

I recognize the immediacy of this situation with people living in the now. I also recognize but don't understand the digital divide that impacts on remote Aboriginal communities in the Northern Territory. Probably elsewhere too. So, I impatiently try to regain my patience and composure. After all, I'm here to help. Phyllis hands me her papers. An overdue notice from the tax department and another scrap piece of paper with some codes – hopefully correct passwords to gain access to her MyGov account. But I soon realise these passwords mean nothing. We get nowhere. Not sure of the spelling of her username, I try a variety of different ways of spelling her name. No luck.

We then start trying adding her Yolngu name, no luck; her totem, no luck; her skin name, no luck. I frustratingly state that you need to be consistent with which name you use and its spelling for official documents and databases. For Yolngu who don't own names like we do, my derision makes no sense.

Eventually, through pure luck I try swapping a letter ›O‹ for a zero and yes! We have cracked the username. Now for the password. Forgotten. Hit the »forgot password« button. The website asks me do I want to send a reset link to a mobile phone number ending in 345 or to Phyllis's email?

»Is that your phone number?« I ask Phyllis.

»›No‹ she says. ›That's an old one‹«.

»What about your email?«

»I don't know the password... I don't know how to use email. You have a look«. Phyllis passes me the phone. It's an android and I am used to an iPhone. It takes me a while to remember the logic. I find the email account. It's open, with dozens of unopened emails. But we don't know the password. Useless. Then I ask if she has another phone. She says no but has another SIM card in her purse. I rejoice and suggest we give that a try. Before Phyllis swaps SIM cards, she checks here Facebook and Instagram feeds. Her phone has been pinging with notifications from the two social media platforms. She changes SIM cards. We try to see if this is linked to her MyGov account. It's not. The phone pings again and again. This time it is for notifications for Facebook, Instagram and TikTok to this other SIM. Phyllis checks these accounts and enjoys a few moments of catching up on family and friend news.

»Do you have any other number?« I ask. She thinks long and hard whilst checking her social media feeds.

»Maybe another SIM card«. She thinks, before pulling FIVE more SIM cards from her wallet! I stare in disbelief while she changes SIM cards in the phone. After four attempts – Bingo! We have a matching number that we can now receive a notification to change the password on Phyllis's MyGov login. I am feeling like we are finally making progress. Phyllis asks me to download the MyGov app on to her phone as she does not have a computer to easily access. I think that is a great idea. She hands me her phone again and this time I notice a game is open and YouTube is playing a video in the background. I close these down to go to the homepage – the homepage wallpaper image is of some men in full customary dress. I install the MyGov app and commence linking the app to her existing account... until we get to the stage of officiating her identification.

Phyllis has her birth certificate. Perfect! Once again, she asks me to enter the information. She does not know what to do. I begin entering her name. I try every conceivable combination of names and their spellings, but the database will not recognize her account to link them together. Ninety-five minutes since they walked into my office, I tell them I have another meeting to go to and Phyllis says okay we can come back tomorrow morning.

I say »Yes, come at 0830 and I will set aside an hour to try and work this out«.

She agrees and leaves, eyes on her phone as it pings merrily away notifying her of her social media updates on a SIM that I have no idea about.

Phyllis didn't show up the following day.

7. Conclusion

Public debate is often the place where new terminology emerges. Initially associated with a specific context, some of it has academic origins, some not. But terminology is appropriated and repurposed. It also gets highly politicised (e.g., »woke« and »fake news«). Some terms are counter-intuitive, such as »populism« – for many people, democracy should be about popular choice, yet this term now carries more cynical connotations that politicians exploit to pivot »the people« against a perceived »establishment« or »elite«. But because many words in English have high utility, combining them into phrases such as »cultural competence« can be problematic. They become even more so when contextualised by the context of the evolving digital environment, a domain that is littered with hybrid tech-speak. This chapter has teased out some of the issues and identified alternative terminology – »intercultural responsiveness« points to where we should head. For us, the way forward is in dialog. This is a space of discovery where words still matter, but they also yield to the spaces in between where listening, reflection, and consideration of other perspectives are valued.

References

Arribas Lozano, A. (2018). Reframing the public sociology debate: Towards collaborative and decolonial praxis. *Current Sociology*, *66*(1), 92–109.

Arroyo, R., Fernández-Lancho, E., & Martínez, E. (2021). Digital Competence in Learning Written Academic Argumentation. *IEEE Revista Iberoamericana de Tecnologias Del Aprendizaje*, *16*(1), 115–121.

Australian Institute for Teaching and School Leadership (AITSL). (2022). *Building a culturally responsive Australian teaching workforce.* https://www.aitsl.edu.au/teach/intercultural-development/building-a-culturally-responsive-australian-teaching-workforce

Badar, F. B. & Mason, J. (2020). Numbers are alarming, solutions are scant – Out of school children in Pakistan. *Proceedings, The International Conference on Sustainable Development 2020 (ICSD2020)*.

Balcazar, F. E., Suarez-Balcazar, Y., & Taylor-Ritzler, T. (2009). Cultural competence: Development of a conceptual framework. *Disability and Rehabilitation*, *31*(14), 1153–1160.

Botelho, M. J., & Lima, C. A. (2020). From Cultural Competence to Cultural Respect: A Critical Review of Six Models. *Journal of Nursing Education*, *59*(6), 311–318.

Branson, D. C. (2020). Student trauma, the hidden curriculum, and cultural humility: This trio needs a team approach. In: Taukeni, S.G. (Ed.), *Addressing multicultural needs in school guidance and counseling* (pp. 82–105). IGI Global.

Burgess, C. (2019). Beyond cultural competence: Transforming teacher professional learning through Aboriginal community-controlled cultural immersion. *Critical Studies in Education*, *60*(4), 477–495.

Canales, M. K. (2000). Othering: Toward an understanding of difference. *Advances in Nursing Science*, *22*(4), 16–31.

Chun, E. & Evans, A. (Eds.) (2016). Rethinking Cultural Competence in Higher Education: An Ecological Framework for Student Development: *ASHE Higher Education Report*, *42*(4). John Wiley & Sons.

Cinelli, M., De Francisci Morales, G., Galeazzi, A., Quattrociocchi, W., & Starnini, M. (2021). The echo chamber effect on social media. *Proceedings of the National Academy of Sciences*, *118*(9), e2023301118.

Coleman, V. (2021). *Digital Divide in UK Education during COVID-19 Pandemic: Literature Review*. Research Report. Cambridge Assessment.

Congdon, D. W. (2022). Deworlded within the World: Bultmann's Paradoxical Politics in an Age of Polarization. *Theology Today*, 79(1), 52–66.

Cope, B. & Kalantzis, M. (2015). Interpreting Evidence-of-Learning: Educational research in the era of big data. *Open Review of Educational Research*, 2(1), 218–239.

Cruz-Jesus, F., Vicente, M. R., Bacao, F., & Oliveira, T. (2016). The education-related digital divide: An analysis for the EU-28. *Computers in Human Behavior*, 56, 72–82.

Danso, R. (2018). Cultural competence and cultural humility: A critical reflection on key cultural diversity concepts. *Journal of Social Work*, 18(4), 410–430.

Daudkhane, Y. (2017). Why SMART Goals are not »Smart« enough? *Imperial Journal of Interdisciplinary Research*. SSRN. 3349004

Dron, J. (2018). Smart learning environments, and not so smart learning environments: a systems view. *Smart Learning Environments*, 5(1), 1–20.

Evans, N., Meñaca, A., Koffman, J., Harding, R., Higginson, I. J., Pool, R., & Gysels, M., on behalf of P., Marjolein. (2012). Cultural Competence in End-of-Life Care: Terms, Definitions, and Conceptual Models from the British Literature. *Journal of Palliative Medicine*, 15(7), 812–820.

Funkhouser, E. (2022). A tribal mind: Beliefs that signal group identity or commitment. *Mind & Language*, 37(3), 444–464.

Gates, B. (1995). *The road ahead*. Penguin: Ringwood, Australia.

Graesser, A. C., Li, H., & Forsyth, C. (2014). Learning by communicating in natural language with conversational agents. *Current Directions in Psychological Science*, 23(5), 374–380.

Grossman, G., Margalit, Y., & Mitts, T. (2022). How the Ultrarich Use Media Ownership as a Political Investment. *The Journal of Politics*, 84(4), 1913–1931.

Hockett, E., Samek, L., & Headley, S. (2012). Cultural humility: A framework for local and global engagement. *International Christian Community of Teacher Educators Journal*, 8(1), 1–13.

Hoel, T. & Mason, J. (2018). Standards for smart education—towards a development framework. *Smart Learning Environments*, 5, 1–25.

Hofstede, G. (2001). *Culture's consequences: Comparing values, behaviors, institutions, and organizations across nations* (2nd Ed.). Sage.

Johnson, Y. M. & Munch, S. (2009). Fundamental Contradictions in Cultural Competence. *Social Work*, 54(3), 220–231.

Kereluik, K., Mishra, P., Fahnoe, C., & Terry, L. (2013). What Knowledge Is of Most Worth. *Journal of Digital Learning in Teacher Education*, 29(4), 127–140.

Koehn, P. H. & Swick, H. M. (2006). Medical Education for a Changing World: Moving Beyond Cultural Competence into Transnational Competence. *Academic Medicine*, 81(6), 548–556.

Kumagai, A. K. & Lypson, M. L. (2009). Beyond Cultural Competence: Critical Consciousness, Social Justice, and Multicultural Education. *Academic Medicine*, 84(6), 782–787.

Li, C., Xing, W., & Leite, W. (2022). Building socially responsible conversational agents using big data to support online learning: A case with Algebra Nation. *British Journal of Educational Technology*, 53(4), 776–803.

Lovari, A. (2020). Spreading (dis)trust: Covid-19 misinformation and government intervention in Italy. *Media and Communication*, 8(2), 458–461.

Luo, M., Hancock, J. T., & Markowitz, D. M. (2022). Credibility perceptions and detection accuracy of fake news headlines on social media: Effects of truth-bias and endorsement cues. *Communication Research*, 49(2), 171–195.

Mari, S., Gil de Zúñiga, H., Suerdem, A., Hanke, K., Brown, G., Vilar, R., Boer, D., & Bilewicz, M. (2022). Conspiracy theories and institutional trust: examining the role of uncertainty avoidance and active social media use. *Political Psychology*, 43(2), 277–296.

Mason, J., Khan, K., & Badar, F. (2021). Making choices during disruption–A resilient digital future for education? In: D. Nanto, M. Rahiem, & T. Maryati (Eds.), Emerging *Trends in Technology for Education in an Uncertain World* (pp. 33–39). Routledge.

Mason, J., Peoples, B. E., & Lee, J. (2020). Questioning the scope of AI standardization in learning, education, and training. *Journal of ICT Standardization*, 8(2) 107–122.

Miller, C. & Bartlett, J. (2012). »Digital fluency«: towards young people's critical use of the internet. *Journal of Information Literacy*, 6(2), 35–55.

Mishra, P. & Mehta, R. (2017). What We Educators Get Wrong About 21st-Century Learning: Results of a Survey. *Journal of Digital Learning in Teacher Education*, 33(1), 6–19.

Nadan, Y. (2017). Rethinking »cultural competence« in international social work. *International Social Work*, 60(1), 74–83.

Norman, H., Adnan, N. H., Nordin, N., Ally, M., & Tsinakos, A. (2022). The Educational Digital Divide for Vulnerable Students in the Pandemic: Towards the New Agenda 2030. *Sustainability*, 14(16), 10332.

Northern Territory Government. (2021). *Education NT Strategy 2021–2025*. https://education.nt.gov.au/__data/assets/pdf_file/0007/1061386/education-NT-strategy-2021-2025.pdf

Ognyanova, K., Lazer, D., Robertson, R. E., & Wilson, C. (2020). *Misinformation in action: Fake news exposure is linked to lower trust in media, higher trust in government when your side is in power*. Harvard Kennedy School Misinformation Review.

Pilon, M. & Brouard, F. (2022). Conceptualizing accountability as an integrated system of relationships, governance, and information. *Financial Accountability & Management*, 39(2), 421–446.

Prensky, M. (2001), Digital Natives, Digital Immigrants Part 1, *On the Horizon*, 9(5), 1–6.

Purnell, L. (2000). A Description of the Purnell Model for Cultural Competence. *Journal of Transcultural Nursing*, 11(1), 40–46.

Purnell, L. D. (2011). *The Purnell Model for Cultural Competence. In Intervention in Mental Health-Substance Use*. CRC Press.

Ragnedda, M. & Muschert, G. W. (2015). *The digital divide: The internet and social inequality in International perspective*. Routledge.

Ray, R. & Davis, G. (2021). Cultural Competence as New Racism: Working as Intended? *The American Journal of Bioethics*, 21(9), 20–22.

Reid, J. A. (2017). Conclusion: Learning the humility of teaching »others«—preparing teachers for culturally complex classrooms. In: C. Reid & J. Major (Eds.), *Global Teaching. Education Dialogues with/in the Global South* (pp. 209–229). Palgrave Macmillan.

Schugurensky, D. & Wolhuter, C. (Eds.) (2020). *Global Citizenship Education in Teacher Education. Theoretical and practical issues*. Routledge.

Shonfeld, M., Cotnam-Kappel, M., Judge, M., Ng, C. Y., Ntebutse, J. G., Williamson-Leadley, S., & Yildiz, M. N. (2021). Learning in digital environments: A model for cross-cultural alignment. *Educational Technology Research and Development*, 69(4), 2151–2170.

Smyrnova-Trybulska, E., Noskova, T., Pavlova, T., Yakovleva, O., & Morze, N. (2016). New educational strategies in contemporary digital environment. *International Journal of Continuing Engineering Education and Life Long Learning*, 26(1), 6–24.

Verhulst, S., Addo, P. M., Young, A., Zahuranec, A. J., Baumann, D., & McMurren, J. (2021). *Emerging Uses of Technology for Development: A New Intelligence Paradigm*. SSRN 3937649.

Williamson, P. (2021). De-Globalisation and decoupling: Post-COVID-19 myths versus realities. *Management and Organization Review*, 17(1), 29209–22934.

Zuboff, S. (2015). Big other: surveillance capitalism and the prospects of an information civilization. *Journal of information technology*, 30(1), 75209–22989.

Digitocracy in the New Normal
Rethinking the Learning Spaces in Higher Education

Stephen D. Bolaji

1. Introduction

In sociological discourse, education performs two functions – manifest and latent functions. Manifest function explains the core responsibility of education
in the context of teaching, research, and community engagement (Kunstler,
2006, p. 33; Julayanont, McFarland & Heilman, 2020). In functionalism theory,
this role is widely acknowledged as an important social institution in sociological discourse for development (Godofsky, Zukin, and Horn, 2011). From medieval to what is now known as 21st century reality, the cardinal objective of
the education sector as the citadel of knowledge and fostering discoveries in
the new area of knowledge has not changed. In the context of knowledge dissemination, research endeavour, and community engagement (Cherrington et
al., 2019). The act of knowing and curiosity to know has been the propelling
force behind human interaction with their environment and social mobility in
society. Bolaji (2010) stressed the manifest function of education as an indispensable tool to man and society for sustainable development. Dewey (1966,
p. 89) also affirmed that through education, society could formulate its purpose, organize its means and resources, and shape itself with definiteness and
economy in the direction it wishes to move. Education must channel all the
individual's intellectual, moral, physical, social, aesthetic, and spiritual potential into a societal ideal (Farayola, 2007). In a nutshell, the manifest function of
education is far-reaching and beyond overemphasizing. Outside the manifest
function, the school has been regarded as the breeding social setting for social
integration, intercultural awareness, and inclusive diversity otherwise known
as the latent function of education. According to Brown-Weinstock (2022), the
social aspect of education makes collaborative practices, inclusive classroom

engagement, and small group dynamics compelling pedagogical approaches in the education sector. This social platform has made the educational setting a place for students to learn about various issues, foster relationships, opportunities for social and political leadership and advocacy, and build skills in relating with people of diverse cultural and socio-economic backgrounds. The descriptive nature of the functions of education is conceptually framed below to deepen understanding of the importance of education as a vehicle of both knowledge and social transformation of society.

2. Conceptual Framework on Functionalism of Education

The conceptual framework of functionalism, as seen in the diagram below (Figure 1), deepens understanding of the manifest and latent functions of school as the avenue that makes an individual become a member of society.

Figure 1: A conceptual framework to deconstruct manifest and latent function of education by the Author.

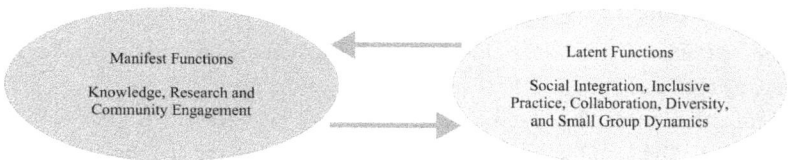

This act is made possible through interface with curriculum knowledge, discoveries of many other ways of acquiring knowledge and exploring the skills gained from knowledge discovery to help the community or society. This manifest function is what Gracia and Levitas (2022) called civic and capital values because of the cash value benefit associated with knowledge acquisition or dissemination. The term »cash value« in this paper alludes to the pragmatism philosophy that refers to the practical usefulness or immediate application of an idea or concept. Pragmatists believe that the value of an idea lies in its ability to solve problems and improve the human condition, rather than in its inherent truth or abstract correctness. The »cash value« of an idea is its tangible, real-world impact, and the results it produces. This emphasis on practicality and utility is a key aspect of pragmatist philosophy. The Durkheim's theory of functionalism provides an overarching understanding of how groups and societies evolve through social interaction (Allen, 2022). This theory is quite relevant to our discussion because it shows the interconnectedness between the two functions of education. More importantly, how through social integration and inclusive practices, knowledge sharing, and teamwork can be productive to attain both individual and group aspirations and goals. The latent function helps to appreciate the cooperative learning approach, project method, and inclusive classroom collaboration that has been the hallmark of the 21st competencies skills in the teaching and learning sector (Merton, 2016). The distinctiveness of the two functions remains the major discourse in sociology of education. Manifest function as righty deconstructed, is a consequence of an action or institution that is intended and recognized by the actors involved. For example, among many pragmatic goals, the manifest function provides education and skills for future employment. The latent function enhances the socialisation of children into the norms and values of society (Merton, 2016). The distinction between latent and manifest functions highlights the importance of considering both the intended and unintended effects of social behaviour and institutions in understanding social reality's complex and multifaceted nature (Merton, 1957). The search for a good society and person has been a consistent effort of various schools of thought, individual philosophers and theologians. These include Plato, Aristotle, Hobbes, Locke, Rousseau, Kant, Hegel, Marx, Illich, and Dewey. This list is not exhaustive. Similarly, the search for a good educational system with all the socio-cultural and intercultural attributes has been the major concern of educational philosophers (Bolaji, Olufowobi & Oluwole, 2013; Bolaji, 2011; Farayola, 2007).

The educational system in any society is influenced by different educational philosophies and philosophical traditions. For instance, the two classical philosophies and their corresponding philosophical traditions that influenced British education were Perennialism and Essentialism. Perennialism is a philosophy that emphasizes the timeless, universal ideas and knowledge that form the foundation of education (Malik, 2021). It believes that these fundamental concepts and skills should form the core curriculum and that education should be focused on passing down this cultural heritage to future generations. In a constructive approach, essentialism is a philosophy of education that emphasizes the acquisition of basic knowledge and skills in core subjects such as reading, writing, and mathematics (Reimer, 2022). It stresses the importance of a structured and disciplined curriculum, as well as the development of character and moral values. Essentialists believe that education should be focused on providing students with the essentials they need to succeed in life (Noddings, 2018). These two philosophies of education have Realism and Idealism, respectively, as their philosophical traditions.

In contemporary times, we have Progressivism and Reconstructionism as educational philosophies that is deeply rooted in Pragmatism upon which the American educational ideology rested (Sleeper, 2001). Pragmatism is a philosophical movement that emphasizes the practical application of ideas and the importance of experience in shaping beliefs and actions. It holds that the truth of a proposition should be judged by its practical usefulness and success, rather than just its logical consistency or correspondence with some external reality (Bolaji, 2011). However, these seem to be the case before and even after the 21st century digital revolution, the higher education sector has been driven by these two functions. The functions have been the driving force behind institutional engagement, and in fact, the core foundation upon which the nexus of engagement between students and teachers rest on (Merton, 2016). That is why breaking from the tradition of classical and didactic practices in knowledge delivery has been a challenge for the traditional higher education sectors whose approaches and modes of operation are firmly rooted in both manifest and latent functions of education skills being encouraged neither in today's educational reform efforts nor in colleges and universities (Merton, 2016; Bolaji, et al, 2013).

Since late 2019, the space of education, especially higher education has witnessed a shift from the traditional narrative to the era of new normal because of the COVID-19 crisis which has had a major impact on the global education sector (Mateen, & Kan, 2021). This paradigm shift has made the space of education an interesting space to work in, with the new systemic level of engagement and operational architecture that has characterized the scope of teacher education offerings globally. The shift has made digitalisation of higher education a necessity. traditional schools were able to adapt to the changing landscape of higher education delivery, but the pandemic has shown the importance of digital infrastructure and support for students in order to ensure that they can continue to learn and succeed during challenging times. Since the classical approach seems to be broken because of the pandemic disruption, navigating a new approach in higher education through online delivery, collaborative ideas, digital learning futures, distance education, and the use of stimulation to cater to some aspects of teacher education is the reality in the current clime (Moyo, 2020; Diaz & Walsh, 2021). It is based on the current reality of the new normal that this chapter takes a critical look at the digitocracy and its nuances in defining the new mode of learning outside the convention of face to face have its impacts and implications. While both online and face-to-face learning have their advantages and disadvantages (Nieves, 2021), parents, teachers, students, and schools need to monitor the new trends to prepare for the future of learning. This chapter acknowledges the need for teachers to refine their methods to create a more engaging online environment for their students. It also recognizes the need for students to leverage the available technologies and use additional study resources (Nieves, 2021).

However, education in the new normal has its pivots and consequences (Scott, 2020). This chapter among many consequences seeks to understand how the manifest and latent functions imbedded in the classical teacher education programs would flourish in this new normal. More importantly, how digital affordances could foster social integration and cultural awareness or intercultural understanding in higher education remains an issue in this chapter. It makes digitocracy of the learning environment a challenge. For emphasis, digitocracy in this chapter is not the term used to describe a political and social system. It is about the influence of digital technology, media, big data, and algorithms on higher education, as well as the unequal distribution of technological resources and skills across different intercultural and social groups in the context of teaching and learning. It is how digital literacy and access to technology can play a key role in fostering intercultural awareness (Reidenberg, 2017). This concept has become increasingly relevant as the use of digital technology has grown in recent years, and as the internet and social media have become major sources of information and political discourse. Hence, the chapter seeks to advocate for a digital learning platform that can make both manifest and latent functions in higher education possible in the learning spaces in the age of the new normal. In addition, digital advocacy to solve the challenge of inequalities and lack of access to digital or online education in the era of pandemics (Duroisin & Tanghe, 2021) is essential. To start this conversation, what is digitoracy in the new normal?

3. Theorising Digitocracy in Higher Education

The word »digitocracy« is a philosophical jargon crafted to subject digitalization to philosophical analysis. Ballesteros (2020) used the word to discuss the concept of power and governance to understand the different layers and manifestations of the act of ruling and being ruled. The word has been used extensively to discuss the impact of digitalization on industrial development and individual lives (Clegg et al., 2023; Dziubina, 2013). For example, digital transformation has a profound effect not only on individual industries but also on value perception. An economy is driven by data no longer emphasizes specific features of a tangible product. Efficiency, convenience, and ease of use are the new currency. In a simple expression, digitalization is seen as a tool for accelerating development in all facets of human endeavors. Also, it has been used interchangeably to connote technologies, technocracy, digital futures, and artificial intelligence (Gulson et al., 2022). In this chapter, digitocracy is a philosophical act of expressing the global revolution evolving through digital technology. This definition is useful to understand how technology has become a tool to demystify the role of humans in all aspects of engagement or interaction (Lumi, 2020). Ballesteros (2020) buttressed the power of digitalization as a way of understanding the inhuman world through strong artificial intelligence (AI). There is hardly any sector of human life including medicine, economy, and political life that digital knowledge has not impacted. This perspective seems to be the new trend, especially in the era of the new normal. Therefore, it is not an exaggeration to say that digitisation has been accepted as the norm for shaping power, society, and humans (Ballesteros, 2020; Cooke, 2021). In a recent research report conducted by Fang Lee Cooke (2021), the project funded by *International Labour Oragnisation* established that digital technology is having a positive impact and is evident in a number of business sectors in terms of changing the nature of their operations. It has become increasingly clear that digitocracy has become the new face of reality globally. In this chapter, it's imperative to understand that digitalisation is not a new phenomenon in pedagogical discourse but has become more relevant in this era of the new normal due to pandemic. What is relatively new in theorising digitalisation is the epistemological standpoint of how this phase of new normal is designed to capture the essence of human engagement, especially in the field of education.

It is not a surprise that the space of education has been caught in this new wave of the digital revolution. The expression of digitalisation, digital classroom, digital literacies, smart classroom, digital pedagogy, and coding have been more amplified by advocates of digitocracy. In fact, the last few years characterized by pandemic, border closure, isolation, and restriction of the movement nationally and internationally have made digitocracy a far more reaching approach to navigating the world of uncertainty. Therefore, rethinking the direction of education pedagogy of engagement in the new normal is a model that is time has come. This new phase has given recognition to the emergence of the 21st century universities with a blended pedagogical approach as a way of learning with a more virtual and digital hybrid to build the nexus between students and teachers (Chambers & Sandford, 2019; Gort & Sembiante, 2015). However, the intricacies that have necessitated the shifts, how the change has impacted knowledge delivery and knowing if further knowledge is needed about this shift are some of the contending issues that are yet unclear. I am aware of the inherent opportunities with digital learning but an understanding of the learning processes and systemic organizations from the perspective of digitalisation and to what extent this has changed when compared with the pre-pandemic conditions means to learners and teachers is something that seems to be well articulated in the body of literature. As the philosophical tradition is, meaning making and making sense is the business of philosophers, (Carr, 2005) discussing the perspectives from both students and teachers in the new era of datafied learning environments remains a fundamental issue yet to be addressed by those advocates of digitocracy. The advantages of digitialisation of the education sector cannot be left unmentioned in this chapter.

4. For Digitorcacy: Supporting the Narrative

Using online platforms as a mode of reaching a wide range of audiences or diverse groups locally and internationally has been the order of the day many school systems. The higher education sector is not an exemption. Even the traditional higher institutions that so heavily relied on face-to-face approach in teaching have embraced the act of digitalisation or digital learning futures. The sector cannot do otherwise with the business model of profit maximization drive that universities are noted for in recent times, especially in Australia that generate over $19 billion as revenue from higher education (Norton, 2014). The digitalisation of the sector for transnational opportunities arguably affirmed the need for the new normal. Digitalisation has been reported in the literature as the vehicle for the deliverables of educational programs across the globe (Hashim, Tlemsani, & Matthews, 2022). Outside the field of teaching and learning, money-making opportunity, managerialism of both the students and teachers is another pointer to digitalization as a necessity in the sector (Deem & Brehony, 2005). Through digital futures, the management of higher education sector can access the productivity of the teachers and students' engagement or interaction. Some digital learning futures like Algorithm, Tableau, and blackboard collaborate are some of that software that are often used to generate such data for decision making process. As with other forms of assessment in higher education, students are also empowered to evaluate their teachers, so, self-evaluation assessment form otherwise known as SELT is commonly used for such assessment. Thus, digitalisation has clearly shown the epistemological transformation of how the stakeholders in the sector are perceived by their supervisors or coordinators (Sadin, 2016). Through digitalisation, the search for individual identity is made possible. To a large extent, the number of realities presented to the managers of education about students, teachers, and other stakeholders in education is virtually infinite according to Ballesteros (2020).

The perspective of technology in teaching and learning is so rich it has become an everyday part of life. This assertion may not appeal to traditional humanism philosophers because of their rationality that is informed by human interaction with the environment and seeking happiness in this life and helping others to achieve the same. However, if we think about the shift and the way in which we make meanings and interact with each other in this contemporary dispensation, we will agree that digitalization of school is essential. Technology is not only enhancing knowledge dissemination and encouraging active participation of the actors in the school system, but it has set a new level of paradigm in communication otherwise known as digital literacies. There are a number of social digital platforms that have proven the legitimacy of digital literacy as relevant against the conventional language skills that the schools are highly noted to enhance in their students. Facebook, Blogs, Twitter, Instagram, We Chat, Gather, and others have consistently redefined literacies beyond the productive and receptive skills focus of the school context. According to Walden (2021), digital language is the trend and other conventional mode of communication is incapacitated to cope with this innovation. The future of language is gradually influenced by modern technological inventions, thereby creating a gap between older people, who cannot keep pace with these advancements, and younger people, leading the digital language evolution. In a nutshell, digitalisation of education is not but stressing its relevance for schools and suggesting ways of enhancing social learning, literacy and literate practices (Carrignton & Robinson, 2009; Walden, 2021).

5. Not Against Digitocracy: But What?

In theorising digitocracy, a number of scholars have reported their reservations about the direction of education in the age of the digital revolution. Some of the thoughts are useful and important for acknowledgment. Some of these reservations are related to reliance on technology as a product engagement in the education context. The work of Floridi et al (2015) gave impetus to the assumption that the analysis of humans as superior to other living organisms is a clear distinction that makes total reliance on digitalization a very blurring concept. In a clearer sense, the work of Ballesteros (2020) that reiterated the concept of human dignity again necessitates the need to seek a deeper meaning of life to know if technology makes the human enigma better. According to Herrmann (2015), there is diversity in our educational environments, including racial and ethnic diversity, linguistic diversity, ability level diversity, and more. Herrmann interprets this as indicating that most classes and schools have undergone a significant change that is likely to persist. As diversity in the classroom and school widens, so does the need for educators to be responsive to diverse student and family needs, beliefs, values, and attitudes. For example, contextual nuances, interpersonal dynamics, emotion and feelings and non-verbal communications are diversity issues that cannot be well captured through digitalization (Cormier, McGrew, Ruble, & Fischer, 2021; Bolaji, et al., 2022). This assertion has provided a contextual narrative of culture as an essential context in the 21st century teaching and learning. To this end, this paper argues that digitalisation of education should be designed to foster cultural competences and culturally responsiveness to cater for the mixed abilities in the classroom setting (Yang, 2021).

The cultural competence awareness in education situates within the sociological discourse of functionalism – manifest and latent functions that higher education is designed to achieve in its learners. The cultural competence awareness in education is situated within the sociological discourse of functionalism in the sense that functionalism views society as a system of interrelated parts that work together to meet the needs of its members and maintain social stability (Zhiming & Wee, 1998). In this context, cultural competence awareness in education is seen as serving the function of promoting social harmony and reducing intercultural conflicts by promoting understanding and respect for diversity. Functionalists argue that education plays an important role in transmitting cultural values and norms to future generations, and that promoting cultural competence awareness is an important aspect of this process. By teaching students to understand and appreciate different cultural perspectives, they are better equipped to navigate diverse social settings and interact effectively with individuals from different backgrounds and as well as to question their cultural bias or perspectives in their relationship with others (Brown-Jeffy & Cooper, 2011; Kalantzis et al., 2016). In this sense, cultural competence awareness in education can be seen as fulfilling a functional need in society by promoting intercultural understanding and reducing conflict, thus contributing to the overall stability and cohesiveness of society. The higher education environment is structured to produce people who are culturally competent and share a variety of attributes. Each of these helps the person to produce better outcomes in the context of rich diversity and understanding of cultural awareness and responsiveness for themselves and others (Kirmayer, 2012). For educators, cultural competence helps students achieve at higher levels and helps students be prepared for college and careers in the 21st century. According to Herrmann (2015), any educator who has been working in the teaching and learning industry for a long time has likely seen the differences between students who were in their classrooms 20 years ago and students who are in their classrooms today. In this vein, I argue that the role of cultural competencies and awareness is apparent in the 21st century teaching and learning just as digitalization of education is as well relevant. Achieving a state of symmetry to accommodate both digital futures and functions (manifest and latent) in higher education would be the ideal way to navigate the age of the new normal. How do we achieve this is the question?

6. Digital – Cultural Pedagogy: The Both ways Approach

The tradition of this both ways approach or pedagogy is more rooted in a blend of both traditional knowledge and western knowledge what Illich called de-schooling society (Michie, Hogue & Rioux, 2018). This premise is to set the tone for a productive blended pedagogical ideal that would connect and foster social imperatives through the aspect of digital futures in teaching and learning. The last three years have witnessed a rise in the number of digital online learning spaces for the dissemination of knowledge. Some of these learning platforms ranging from Blackboard Collaborate, Gather, Google, Codecademy, Moodle, Pluralsight, Skillshare, Coursera, Teachable, and others have made the acquisition of knowledge through the online platform easy and effective. What they have failed to achieve is how the social imperatives attributes of functionalism in higher education can be enacted to cater to the interpersonal relationship of both the learners and teachers in the industry. The social imperatives in the context of this paper are cultural awareness, the value of diversity, responding to cross-cultural differences, learning about students' cultures, and making positive changes. Fostering these imperatives seems to be lacking in the current structure of the online platforms (Bolaji, et al. 2022).

The importance of digitalisation of higher education cannot be overemphasized. As mentioned in the introduction section of this chapter, many scholars have reported the inherent opportunity towards the digital transformation of the universities that seems to have a positive effect on the teaching methods (Zawacki-Richter, 2021), improving the quality of education (Rodríguez-Abitia et al., 2000) and the need to move between embodied and digitalized forms of learning towards an integral pedagogy (Aroles and Küpers, 2021). From the managerialism perspective as well, digitocracy has been accepted as the new normal because of the potential opportunity for creativity and innovation in the educational experience, cultivating the desirable entrepreneurial spirit within the academic communities (Ratten, 2020). Developing blended pedagogies, particularly in relation to social imperatives, literacy practices, and digital learning futures would make the space of learning futures (Mehta and Aguilera, 2020). That is devoid of that social inequality for an educational pedagogy that promotes humanism traditions in teaching and learning (Foucault, 1984; Mehta & Aguilera, 2020). The drive for a blended approach largely is based on the concern of the educational stakeholders who believe that education is about social integration and that people are the center of any educational outcomes. Hence it can be argued that digitalisation is a pedagogy and social imperatives is also a pedagogy on their own. Therefore, both must connect to have a holistic digitocracy as a way of life in the 21st century education. Thus, social imperatives are not only drivers for a digital pedagogy but also pedagogical imperatives (Howell, 2012; Castanẽta & Selwyn, 2018; Means, 2019; Grange, 2020; Tavin, 2021).

A preliminary report from a study on »virtual learning and cultural awareness in higher education« by three colleges of education in Germany, Australia, and Israel in 2020 revealed the need for a constructive connection between educational perspectives and socialisation against the narrative of hybrid digitality and datafied realities. Making sense of digital learning in connection with social imperatives has the potential to enhance epistemological intervention in digitalization of education. The proposition in this paper is a blended pedagogy captured in the framework below (figure 2) as the most effective way for both teachers and students upon which knowledge and functionalism of education rest.

Figure 2: *Proposed blended pedagogy for engagement in the new normal drawn from Howell (2012) thoughts on digitalization of education.*

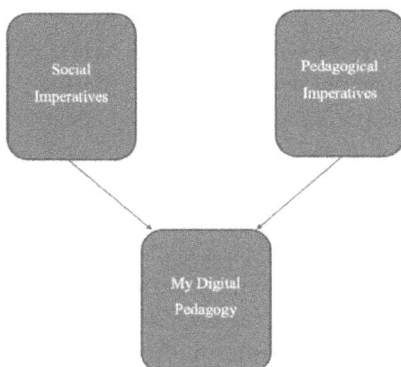

With this framing of the role of digitocracy in education, how can teachers whose didactic approach and epistemological engagement or knowledge delivery is rooted in face-to-face pedagogy imbibe digital pedagogy as a new normal for knowledge dissemination? Pedagogy as widely defined is the study of being a teacher and the act of teaching (Howell, 2012; Shirke, 2021). Beyond the literary definition as a method of teaching, pedagogy shapes teaching beliefs and understanding of culture and different learning styles. More importantly, it is the essential components for meaningful classroom relationships for both students and teachers (Shirke, 2021). The emphasis on social integration in a classroom setting is achievable through the instrumentality of pedagogical techniques. With the digital revolution, there is a need for advocates of digitalisation to look beyond the opportunities that digital affordances offer to accommodate the structural functionalism of social integration and that makes face to face pedagogy a compelling approach for learners (Parsons, Inkila, & Lynch, 2019). Currently, the digital learning platforms are yet to capture the latent functions of engagement in higher as they should to promote that rich intercultural understanding and diversity dynamics which is the position of this chapter. Arguably, I understand the nature of digital technologies is fast-changing and evolving, desire to have digital learning spaces to cater to social inclusion, intercultural relationship, and diversity enrichment (Wellstead, 2017), learners and teachers should be the focus of education in the new normal.

7. Conclusion

This chapter leverage on the understanding that the last few years can be seen as the era of a new normal because of the COVID-19 crisis which has had a major impact on the global education sector (Mateen, & Kan, 2021). This new normal has made space of education an interesting space to work because of the systemic level of engagement and operational architecture that has characterized the scope of teacher education offerings globally. The engagement in the new normal necessitated a wide range of strategies ranging from online delivery, collaborative ideas, digital learning futures, distance education, and the use of simulation to cater to some aspects of teacher education has been widely discussed in the body of literature (Moyo, 2020; Diaz, & Walsh, 2021). As argued in the chapter, the new approach fostered the narrative of digitoracy as a new mode of learning outside the convention of face-to-face pedagogy that we are familiar with. As it has its impacts and implications (Nieves, 2021), teachers, students, and schools need to monitor the new trends to prepare for the future of learning. The chapter discussed how digital learning has been an effective pedagogy in meeting the manifest function of education in knowledge dissemination and research engagement, but the latent function seems to be neglected, which in a sense makes the whole essence of higher education a one-sided (Fischer, Lundin, & Lindberg, 2020). In this paper, I explore the nuances of digitalization from both side of the same coin and concluded that virtual and digital tool has come to stay as the mode of engagement in the 21st century teaching and learning. However, any digital affordances that cannot foster social integration and cultural awareness or intercultural understanding in higher education make digitocracy of the learning environment a challenge. Hence, there is a need for digital learning platform to make both manifest and latent functions in higher education possible in the learning spaces in the age of the new normal.

References

Aguilera-Hermida, A.P. (2020). College students' use and acceptance of emergency online learning due to COVID-19. *International Journal of Educational Research Open*, 1(100011), https://doi.org/10.1016/j.ijedro.2020.100011

Aroles, J. & Küpers, W. (2021). Towards an integral pedagogy in the age of »digital Gestell«: moving between embodied co-presence and telepresence and telepresence in learning and teaching practices. *Management Learning*, 53(5), https://doi.org/10.1177/13505076211053871

Ballesteros, A. (2020). Digitocracy: Ruling and Being Ruled. *Philosophies*, 5(2), 9. http://dx.doi.org/10.3390/philosophies5020009

Bolaji, S.D. & Pollock, Wayne (2022) Where is philosophy of education in teacher education in Australia? In: S.D. Bolaji, A. Oni., & S. Anyama, (Eds.), *African Education and Diaspora Studies* (pp. 1–11). Charles Darwin University Press.

Bolaji, S.D., Bohmer, A., Gromick, N., & Anyama, S. (2022). *Management of Teacher Education Program in The New Normal: A Comparative and Explorative Study*. Seminar Paper. Northern Institute, Charles Darwin University (14 July 2022).

Bolaji, S.D., Olufowobi, O.O., & Oluwole, S.K (2013). Reinventing the wheel of progress in Nigerian Education: Deweyian Perspective. *Journal of Educational Management*, 1(2), 167–176.

Bolaji S.D (2011) *Dewey's Philosophy and Contemporary Education in Nigeria: Implications for Democracy and Education*. Ph.D Unpublished Thesis Submitted to the School of Postgraduate Studies, University of Lagos. URI: https://ir.unilag.edu.ng/handle/123456789/4210

Brown-Jeffy, S. & Cooper, J. E. (2011). Toward a conceptual framework of culturally relevant pedagogy: An overview of the conceptual and theoretical literature. *Teacher education quarterly*, 38(1), 65–84.

Brown-Weinstock (2022). Theoretical Perspectives on Education. retrieved https://courses.lumenlearning.com/suny-fmcc-intro-to-sociology/chapter/theoretical-perspectives-on-education/

Carr, D. (2005). *Making sense of education: An introduction to the philosophy and theory of education and teaching*. Routledge.

Carrington, V. & Robinson, M. (Eds.) (2009). *Digital literacies: Social learning and classroom practices*. SAGE Publications Ltd, https://dx.doi.org/10.4135/9781446288238

Chambers, F. & Sandford, R. (2019). Learning to be human in a digital world: a model of values fluency education for physical education. *Sport, Education and Society*, 24(9), 925–938. https://doi.org/10.1080/13573322.2018.1515071

Cherrington, A. M., Scheckle, E., Khau, M., De Lange, N., & Du Plessis, A. (2019). What does it mean to be an »engaged university«? Reflections from a university and school-community engagement project. *Education, Citizenship and Social Justice*, 14(2), 165–178.

Clegg, S., Simpson, A. V., Cunha, M. P., & Rego, A. (2023). From »leadership« to »leading«: power relations, polyarchy and projects. *The SAGE Handbook of Leadership* (pp. 395–405). SAGE Publications Ltd.

Cooke, F. L., Bamber, G., Jerrard, M., McKeown, T., Pittard, M., Tyvimaa, T., & Drogemuller, R. (2021). *New Technologies, the Future of Work, Skills and Industrial Relations (IR).* https://research.monash.edu/en/projects/new-technol ogies-the-future-of-work-skills-and-industrial-relatio

Cormier, McGrew, J., Ruble, L., & Fischer, M. (2021). Socially distanced teaching: The mental health impact of the COVID-19 pandemic on special education teachers. *Journal of Community Psychology*, 50(3), 1768–1772. https://d oi.org/10.1002/jcop.22736

Dewey, J. (1916/1966). *Democracy and education.* New York: Macmillan.

Deem, R. & Brehony, K. J. (2005). Management as ideology: The case of »new managerialism« in higher education. *Oxford review of education*, 31(2), 217–235. https://doi.org/10.1080/03054980500117827

Diaz, M.C.G. & Walsh, B. M. (2021). Telesimulation – based education during COVID-19. *The Clinical Teacher*, 18(2), 121–125. https://doi.org/10.1111/tct.13 273

Duroisin, N., Beauset, R., & Tanghe, C. (2021). Education and digital inequalities during COVID-19 confinement: From the perspective of teachers in the French speaking Community of Belgium. *European Journal of Education*, 56(4), 515–535. https://doi.org/10.1111/ejed.12475

Dziubina, O. (2013). The influence of internet-related affixes on the formation of computer neologisms and on the emergence of the new concepts. *Science And World*, 148.

Falaiye, M. (2007). Democratic Value and Role of the Youth. In: T. Ebijuwa (Ed.), *Philosophy and Social Change. Discourse on Values in Africa* (pp. 173). Hope Publication Limited.

Farayola, J.A. (2007). *Kantian idea of autonomy and democratic education in Nigeria.* Ph.D Unpublished Thesis, University of Ibadan.

Fischer, G., Lundin, J., & Lindberg, J. O. (2020). Rethinking and reinventing learning, education and collaboration in the digital age – from creating technologies to transforming cultures. *International Journal of Information and Learning Technology*, 37(5), 241–252. https://doi.org/10.1108/IJILT-04-2 020-0051

Floridi, L., Cowls, J., Beltrametti, M., Chatila, R., Chazerand, P., Dignum, V., Luetge, C., Madelin, R., Pagallo, U., Rossi, F., Schafer, B., Valcke, P., & Vayena, E. (2018). *AI4People – An Ethical Framework for a Good AI Society: Opportunities, Risks, Principles, and Recommendations*. Atomium; European Institute for Science, Media and Democracy.

Foucault, M. (1984) Polemics, Politics, and Problemizations: An Interview with Michel Foucault. In: Rabinow, P. (Ed.), *The Foucault Reader* (pp. 381–390). Penguin.

Godofsky, J., Zukin, C., & Van Horn, C. (2011). *Unfulfilled Expectations: Recent College Graduates Struggle in a Troubled Economy*. Rutgers University.

Gort, M. & Sembiante, S.F. (2015). Navigating Hybridized Language Learning Spaces Through Translanguaging Pedagogy: Dual Language Preschool Teachers' Languaging Practices in Support of Emergent Bilingual Children's Performance of Academic Discourse. *International Multilingual Research Journal*, 9(1), 7–25. https://doi.org/10.1080/19313152.2014.981775

Garcia, K. & Levitas J. (2022). *What is the Role of School?* https://study.com/learn /lesson/manifest-function-education-concept-examples.html

Gulson, K.N., Sellar, S., & Webb, P. T. (2022). *Algorithms of Education: How Datafication and Artificial Intelligence Shape Policy*. University of Minnesota Press.

Hashim, M.A.M., Tlemsani, I., & Matthews, R. (2022). Higher education strategy in digital transformation. *Education and Information Technologies*, 27, 3171–3195. https://doi.org/10.1007/s10639-021-10739-1

Herrmann, E. (2015). *Cultural competence in the classroom: A key 21st-century skill*. Retrieved 2022 https://exclusive.multibriefs.com/content/cultural-compe tence-in-the-classroom-a-key-21st-century-skill/education

Howell, J. (2012). *Teaching with ICT: Digital Pedagogies for Collaboration and Creativity*. Melbourne, Victoria: Oxford University Press.

Jandrić, P. (2019). Ewa Mazierska, Leslie Gillon, & Tony Rigg (Eds.), Popular Music in the Post-Digital Age: Politics, Economy, Culture and Technology: 304 Pp. New York and London: Bloomsbury, 2019 (ISBN: 978-1-5013-3837-3). *Postdigital Science and Education*, 1(1), 247–251. https://doi.org/10.1007/s4 2438-018-0016-5

Jandrić, P. (2017). *Learning in the Age of Digital Reason.* Sense Publishers. https://doi.org/10.1007/978-94-6351-077-6

Julayanont, P., McFarland, N.R., & Heilman, K.M. (2020). Mild cognitive impairment and dementia in motor manifest Huntington's disease: Classification and prevalence. *Journal of the Neurological Sciences, 408,* 116523–116523. https://doi.org/10.1016/j.jns.2019.116523

Kalantzis, M., Cope, B., Chan, E., & Dalley-Trim, L. (2016). *Literacies.* Cambridge University Press.

Kaleigh A. (2022). *Understand functionalism, a theory advanced by sociologist Emile Durkheim. Learn his observations on the division of labor, anomie, and solidarity in society.* https://study.com/academy/lesson/emile-durkheims-theories-functionalism-anomie-and-division-of-labor.html

Kirmayer, L.J. (2012). Rethinking cultural competence. *Transcultural Psychiatry,* 49(2), 149–164. doi:10.1177/1363461512444673

Kunstler B. (2006). The millennial University, then and now: from late medieval origins to radical transformation. *On the Horizon,* 14(2), 62–69. https://doi.org/10.1108/10748120610674021

Le Grange, L. (2020). Could the COVID-19 pandemic accelerate the uberfication of the university. *South African Journal of Higher Education,* 34(4), 1–10. http://dx.doi.org/10.20853/34-4-4071.

Lumi, A. (2020). The Impact of Digitalisation on human resources development. *Prizren Social Science Journal,* 4(3), 39–46. https://doi.org/10.32936/pssj.v4i3.178

Malik, J. (2021). Philosophy of Perennialism and Its Relevance to Contemporary Islamic Education. *Ri'ayah: Jurnal Sosial dan Keagamaan,* 6(01), 84–94.

Means, A.J. (2019). Platform urbanism, creativity, and the new educational futurism. *Education Theory,* 69(2), 205–223.

Mehta, R. & Aguilera, E. (2020). A critical approach to humanizing pedagogies in online teaching and learning. *International Journal of Information and Learning Technology,* 37(3), 109–120. https://doi.org/10.1108/IJILT-10-2019-0099

Merton, R. (2016). Manifest and latent functions. In: *Social Theory Re-Wired* (pp. 68–84). Routledge.

Merton, R. K. (1957). *Social theory and social structure.* Free Press.

Noddings, N. (2018). Philosophy of education. 4th Ed. Routledge.

Norton, A. (2014). *Mapping Australian higher education 2014–15.* Grattan Institute.

Parsons, D., Inkila, M., & Lynch, J. (2019). Navigating learning worlds: Using digital tools to learn in physical and virtual spaces. *Australasian Journal of Educational Technology*, *35*(4). https://doi.org/10.14742/ajet.3675

Ratten, V. (2020). Coronavirus (COVID-19) and the entrepreneurship education community. *Journal of Enterprising Communities*, *14*(5), 753–764. https://doi.org/10.1108/JEC-06-2020-0121

Rodríguez-Abitia, G., Martínez-Pérez, S., Ramirez-Montoya, M.S., Lopez-Caudana, E. (2020). Digital Gap in Universities and Challenges for Quality Education: A Diagnostic Study in Mexico and Spain. *Sustainability*, *12*(21), 9069. https://doi.org/10.3390/su12219069

Reidenberg, J.R. (2017). Digitocracy. *Communications of the ACM*, *60*(9), 26–28. https://doi.org/10.1145/3126489

Reimer, B. (2022). *A philosophy of music education: Advancing the vision.* 3rd Ed. State University of New York Press.

Sadin, E. (2016). *La Siliconisation du Monde : L'irrésistible Expansion du Libéralisme Numérique.* L'échappée.

Shirke, A. (2021). *What Is Pedagogy? Importance Of Pedagogy in Teaching and Learning Process.* https://www.iitms.co.in/blog/importance-of-pedagogy-in-teaching-and-learning-process.html

Sleeper, R.W. (2001). *The necessity of pragmatism: John Dewey's conception of philosophy.* University of Illinois Press.

Snyder, D.P. (Ed.) (2006). *Post industrial University.* Emerald Publishing Limited.

Steiner, D. M. (1994). *Rethinking Democratic Education: The Politics of Reform.* The John Hopkins University Press.

Tavin, K., Kolb, G., & Tervo, J. (Eds.) (2021). *Post-Digital, Post-Internet Art and Education: The Future Is All-Over.* Palgrave Macmillan. https://doi.org/10.1007/978-3-030-73770-2

Walden, V.C. (2021). Understanding Holocaust memory and education in the digital age: before and after Covid-19. *Holocaust Studies*, *28*, 257–278. https://doi.org/10.1080/17504902.2021.1979175

Wellstead, P. (2017). Information Cultures in the Digital Age: A Festschrift in Honor of Rafael Capurro. In: M. Kelly & J. Bielby (Eds.) (2016). *Journal of Education for Library and Information Science*, *58*(1), 44–45. https://doi.org/10.3138/jelis.58.1.44

Yang, W. (2021). Glocalisation, digitalisation & curriculum hybridisation. *Research Intelligence*, *148*(3), 24–25.

Zawacki-Richter, O. (2021). The current state and impact of COVID-19 on digital higher education in Germany. *Human Behavior and Emerging Technologies*, 3(1), 218–226. https://doi.org/10.1002/hbe2.238

Zhiming, B. & Wee, L. (1998). Functionalism in education: A critique of the communicative approach to language teaching. *Text in Education and Society*, 91–105. https://doi.org/10.1142/9789812815781_0006

Digital Bodies
On Signification, Learning, and Embodiment
in Digital Teaching

Anselm Böhmer

Social and cultural categories have long been seen as combined with the bodily »habitus« and its relevance for societal positions (Bourdieu, 1984; Foucault, 1988). In these approaches, the performance of the body is considered essential for socializing individuals in modern societies. Therefore, bodily performance as »habitus« is a relevant factor regarding social interactions and the social positioning of individuals and groups. Moreover, culture affects the embodied expression of social positions and concepts – the habitus serves as an indicator of social differences or even as a basis of discrimination (Brubaker, 2004; Hall, 1996). Additionally, digital performance has become a relevant form of interacting with others. Since the pandemic, digital performance has started to affect teaching as a new common form of interaction in higher education (Böhmer et al., 2022) and has also become a relevant factor in socializing the participants within their academic fields.

In this paper, two dynamics of modern societies are reflected on and considered together: culturalization and digitalization. Both developments lead to the question of what has happened to the two fields mentioned above, i.e., social embodment by cultural positioning and by (further) digitalizing higher education. This paper thus deals with the following questions: What characterizes embodment in a digital learning environment? What educational consequences does this have for future education in digital learning environments? To find answers to these questions, this article describes how significatory processes can be conceptualized (1). In the next step, cultural significations are explained in the field of culturalization (2) and with regard to learning as the embodied production of social meaning (3). Finally, these findings illustrate how and to what extent culture and digitality are shaping the process from meaning to sense-making in modern societies (4) – and thus in current higher education.[1]

1. Signification

Social processes depend on the habitus, i.e., appearance, behavior, performance, and distinction of an individual and thus on her*his embodiment (Bourdieu, 1984; Bourdieu & Passeron, 1990).[2] In this way, actors are embedded in the cultural structures of the particular field. One of these fields, especially relevant for higher education, is the learning environment students work in. In the first approach to social and cultural aspects of digital learning environments, a differentiated understanding of what it means to address someone as a member of something is needed to understand the social structures that occur here. Therefore, practices of description and addressing need to be deconstructed.

First, the critical change structuralism brought into sciences has to be considered. When Saussure (1989) analyzed language and its use, he described the relation of signifiers to each other as crucial for understanding. In this view, the meaning and the sense of something are not »given« by the signifier – but produced by the signifier and its relation to other signifiers. Language becomes a dynamic practice of signification, identification, power, and difference (Laclau, 2006, pp. 36ff.).

Applied to the challenges facing the individual and its subjectivizing relations, this can be interpreted as saying that the subject is created by the relations of signifiers addressing the individual. The consequence of this shift in social sciences is a »decentering of the subject« (Beer & Sievi, 2010). On the

---

1   This paper was made possible due to funding of two projects by the German Academic Exchange Service (DAAD): DIVA – Digital and International Virtual Academic Cooperation (Project-ID: 57564212) in 2020 and 2021, and EUGEN – Educational Systems, Global Competencies and Education 4.0 (Project-ID: 57598276) in 2021 and 2022.

2   As this reception of social theory shows, this paper's standpoint is neither phenomenological nor psychoanalytical, but is to be understood simply and plainly as a social constructivist theory of learning (Böhmer, 2016). Virtuality is thus not conceptualized here as a mere mental performance of an individual, but as a responsive practice (Waldenfels, 1994) within the field created by the embodied subject, digital learning environment, and the dynamics between the two (for more details on the strangeness of embodiment: Waldenfels, 2022, pp. 158ff.).

other hand, one can discover a structural openness of subjectivity to social and political attitudes that determine the manner and framework of address and reference.

The notions of knowledge, meaning, and sense need to be carefully differentiated (Posselt & Flatscher, 2018, p. 62) in a way that shows the construction of these epistemological relations. Various modes of signification occur when these relations are manifested in socio-linguistic interactions (for their »ideological« structure, cf. Hall, 1982). Among these are aural, visual, gestural, tactile, spatial, spoken, and written practices, as well as their layouts (Magnusson & Godhe, 2019). In this context, Kress (2010) describes aspects of socio-semiotic multimodality as »the result of a social and historical shaping of materials chosen by a society for representation« (ibid., p. 11). He clarifies that language modes result from social and historical frames and processes. Hence they are as arbitrary as a language but also relevant for the individual with its self- and world-relation called »subjectivity.«

For anyone to understand any undefined thing in a specific sense, the modes of language used for signification in a social interaction must manifest coherence of meaning. Neither the signified (as mentioned above) nor the signifiers are relevant in creating meaning. Nevertheless, the conceptualization of relations between signifiers is framed by specific forms and dynamics of their environment. As this coherence is achieved in social interactions, these social dynamics lead to »a more dynamic understanding, according to which coherence is conceptualized as a potentially variable co-operative achievement of the speaker/writer and the hearer/reader and seen as a context-dependent, hearer/reader-oriented and comprehension-based, interpretative notion« (Haase et al., 2007, p. 6). This cooperative understanding needs not only to be developed through language but can also be realized through material collaboration (Chen et al., 2021, p. 169). Thus, this meaningful coherence is not a static and finalized entity but situated within social processes and their variations. From this perspective, a socio-semiotic coherence produces »situated knowledges« (Haraway, 1988) and variations of the »same« so that iterations (Derrida, 1982) occur in the performance of meaning. Thus, every objectivity is infused with dynamic variations that do not allow a precisely fixed meaning; instead, objectivity is related to the meaning-making process of the subject and its perception.

Regarding social identity, this concept demonstrates the relevance of the subject's signification as an expression of general linguistic practice.[3] Because all members of a language community engage in almost the same linguistic practice (and its distinct differences), the individuals perform on a common ground of reality and meaning by participating in the same common practice of linguistic expression. A »community of linguistic practice« (following Lave & Wenger, 1991) occurs. Thus their identifying behavior, such as »A is one of us, but B is not,« expresses the social order of belonging and identity. Consequently, social belonging (or exclusion) is not an outcome of objectively given facts or subjectively committed attitudes, but the meaning of specific uses of semiotic resources and in addressing oneself and others. Addressing, therefore, leads to belonging and expulsion, inclusion and exclusion, framed by particular meaning-making of social groups.

Such an identity – that is group-oriented as well as field-specific – does not go beyond addressing somebody as someone. To be able to do this addressing, a speaker needs specific terms. »I am not doing away with the category, but trying to relieve the category of its foundationalist weight to render it as a site of permanent political contest.« (Butler, 1992, p. 8) In this view, signifying takes on a double meaning – as social practice, signification opens up the possibilities of belonging, and as a political practice, signification requires a specific relation to power. The category is thus the »nodal point« (Laclau & Mouffe, 2013) of discourses and social identity, belonging, and hegemony.

Kress specifies: »(1) that *signs are motivated conjunctions of form and meaning*; that conjunction is based on (2) *the interest of the sign-maker*; using (3) *culturally available resources*.« (Kress, 2010, p. 10) Thus we can understand this view as rooted in a social and power-related perspective: addressing is led by interest and formed by culture but connects individuals as groups by granting them a specific subjectivity (and rules out other types) within the particular field. Social identity as an outcome of a socio-semiotic approach is thus neither an individual nor a social score but a linguistic and cultural result. Hence, identity as social meaning is a threefold performance of logic regarding addresser, signifier, and addressed (following the communication theory of Lehmann-Rommel, 2015, p. 68).

---

3   For the relevance of culture to identity production, cf. paragraph 2.2 of this article.

2. Culture and Culturalization

2.1 The Term and its Capital

»Culture« is a term that is often used in global and international education projects. To give a short description regarding the societal phenomenon of culturality (here following Hall, 1996, 1997): The term *culture* describes a wide range of practices, customs, habits, and sets of meanings[4] formed by and based on historical, social, and power-related conditions of perspectives on hegemony, subordination, and resistance (for political aspects of this approach cf. Kruse, 2022, pp. 100ff.). Hegemonical and subordinated positions result from the culturalization of social differences, defined as »cultural differences« that matter in the particular field and its significatory aspects of the language classifying and framing this field (Hall, 1982). Thus, Hall brings together everyday practices on the micro level of society and structural perspectives on the macro level (Davis, 2004, p. 162). In doing this, he describes a norm of »Western« culture for social relations as well as for international contacts, producing hierarchies in terms of cultural attributions, and finds separation from the non-Western »Rest« (Hall, 1996).

This has at least two consequences for the question discussed here: First, culture is not only a term to describe traditions or officially acknowledged customs, but one that should comprise reference to every single practice performed by communities – and individuals as well. The cultural relevance of individual practices lies first in their performance of collective cultural protocols and their significance as »environmental elements« for community practices. In realizing a community's »culture«, individuals never perform those common practices, customs, habits, and sets of meanings twice in the same way, as has already been established with regard to Derrida's (1982) »différance.« Individual cultural performance is never the exact recapitulation of common cultural elements and prescriptions. Every single practice can

---

4   With this term, I would like to make a critical reference to the more often used concept of »values«. These values seem to mark a certain signification in social, cultural, and political discourses. But quite often they do not lead to specific, »value-oriented« practice, as has been shown for many cases in Western migration debates. These concepts therefore do not seem to value a certain perspective, behaviour, and political attitude, but to be signifiers in the aforementioned discourses that are as useful as »empty« (Laclau, 2006). Their emptiness is also the reason that the common debate on them does not seem to address sense, but meaning only (for more details cf. paragraph 4.3).

thus be seen as cultural practice in itself and embedded in a network of other cultural performances and structures.

Second, culture is often used in modern societies to mark differences. Culture is described as one form of capital (Bourdieu, 1986) that helps or obstructs social positionings. Culture also functions as a signifier of exclusion. This kind of social application occurs in the clarification of whether a given individual or a group shares the common ground of »us« or if they are »them«, the »others.« This form of »*othering* the different« (Böhmer, 2020a) can be described in its culturalized form as a particular version of signification (Böhmer, 2020b, pp. 177ff.). A particular speech or text therefore not only describes facts or articulates the speaker's self but also forms a relationship between the speaker/writer, the hearer/reader, and the object discussed. Both social partners in the textual relation, i.e., the speaker/writer and the hearer/reader, seem to depend on each other. That is, the one self in its identity seems to vanish without the other: »This [...] necessity of the Other to the self, this inscription of identity in the look of the other finds its articulation profoundly in the ranges of a given text.« (Hall, 1997, p. 48) The text, whether spoken or written, marks anyone as someone and, at the same time, defines this »someone's« position in the particular social field, in relation to the others there.

This signification frames and pre-structures social identities and fields, but it is also historically and politically framed (Hall, 1997). Culture, therefore, is not only a term that describes human practices but also addresses the relation between power and subordination, inclusion and exclusion, and acknowledgment and disregard.

2.2 Social Constructivism

The previous reconstructions of socio-semiotic practices make clear that signifying practices do not lead to any kind of essentialism but to the verbal effects of addressing, identifying, and constructing. In the approach of cultural signification, social processes are constructed and performed within a particular field of language and identity.

Signifying practices and linguistically transmitted sets of meanings need to be considered more profoundly to understand the process of constructing social relations and societal realities by signifying anyone as someone. The reason for this reflection on language and sets of meanings in social practices is that language rests on those sets of meanings and reproduces them by defining a person as a specific individual. As Althusser (2001) shows: Shouting »Hey, you there!« makes someone a specifically identified figure – e.g., the thief others are forced to address as a threat – and through this as a person in a particular social position. Therefore, cultural capital – as well as structural and symbolic (Bourdieu, 1986) – leads people to their individual and social opportunities of self-determination in »reified or living« forms such as embodied, objectified, or institutionalized statuses (ibid.). Being addressed as a member of a cultural group means being seen not only as an element of cultural practices but at the same time as connected to certain types of bodily appearance, being connected to particular cultural objects, or being placed at specific positions in an institution. This does not determine the individual in an absolute way but defines those spaces the individual is forced to find an answer to (Waldenfels, 1994). Thus, culturalization ascribes not only groupist identities (Brubaker, 2004) but also creates individual subjectivity.

Furthermore, cultural capital helps first and foremost in the meaning-making of a situation and all those who participate in it. Cultural capital signifies and produces the meaning of individuals as well as of particular objects or knowledge in the specific field. To give an example: the dress of an individual signifies not only fashion preferences and functional necessities but also the adequacy of representational appropriateness relative to a given or required social position within a particular social field (Bourdieu, 1984; for the field of education, classically, Bourdieu & Passeron, 1990). In this way, a specific social meaning is created by the situation, the individuals, and their behavior; but what is also conveyed is the meaning of this situation for the field in general: Is this guy dressed appropriately? Is s*he presenting their social role, relevance, and importance as would be expected? What does it mean if somebody appears like this? And so on. Invariably, a particular cultural significance is relevant for the emergence of a specific, field- and situation-related meaning for the individual, the other participants, and the situation itself.

Second, a particular instance of social reality not only means something to be understood; cultural capital also opens up the portals of »sense«, i.e., more complex thinking that »require[s] reasoning, reflection, and analysis« (Mason, 2014, p. 207) to create the cohesion of different emerging meanings in the particular social reality. There is not only a practice of signification at work here; even more than this, it is the relevance of functional interaction between individuals, groups, and classes – and culture thus becomes an active process of emerging meaning and sense (Scherr, 2012, pp. 321f.).

From this perspective, a concept of culture emerges that refers to the situated practices of individuals and requires their field- and self-determined interactions in the particular situation to develop meaning and, resulting from this, sense (for more details, see paragraph 4) with regard to their meaning-constructions and the more complex sense-creations.

2.3 Culturalized Discrimination

Stuart Hall describes »The West and the Rest« (Hall, 1996) as the epitome of a divided society where culture defines positions and grades of freedom of different groups – the »others« (ibid., pp. 205ff.) are the marginalized and low-powered groups of those who are addressed as culturally different. According to Hall, discrimination and culture work hand in hand: Where »others« are performed in cultural practices, pushed to the margins, and get less power, they are discriminated. As previously shown, language plays a significant role in »othering« the »othered« – by marking their differences with signifiers that assign them to specific structures of the field and map out for them a distinct and differently equipped position within it.

Following Hall further, we can use his signifying approach to deconstruct the terminological othering that is taking place in this context. He delineates a number of common strategies:

> »1 idealization;
> 2 the projection of fantasies of desire and degradation;
> 3 the failure to recognize and respect difference;
> 4 the tendency to impose European categories and norms, to see difference through the modes of perception and representation of the West.« (Hall, 1996, p. 215)

This first amounts to a hegemonial request by a colonialistic region of the world (»the West«[5]) that essentially does not reflect on colonialist practices. As a result, the colonialistic approach leads to discriminating practices in

---

5   This term is used by Hall not to describe a topographic region or continent, but to mark cultural-historic practices and policies. In recent developments such as the Russian war on Ukraine, colonialist attitudes in politics and culture are obviously not located in a topographic sense in »the West«.

the everyday lives of many people.[6] Therefore, cultural discrimination is not only an active hazard but also a subversive everyday experience and societal practice. Hence discriminating significations do not only mean disrespectful behavior on the part of the »discriminators« and offended self-esteem among those who are culturally othered. In addition, discriminating significations occur systematically in many everyday situations and fields – including that of education.

How these discriminations occur in the »new normal«[7] field of digitalization after »the COVID-19 pandemic and the resulting suspension of face-to-face activities in schools and universities across the world« (Willat & Flores, 2022, p. 22), will be explained in the following paragraph.

3. Digitality

The term digitality marks a cultural shift and expresses an essential social and subjective signifier relating to recent changes in societal structures. This term will be defined here and used to reflect on culturalized addressing as a specific phenomenon in education.

3.1 Digitalization and Digitality

The term »digitalization« describes the process of transferring an analogical medium into a digital one, like scanning a book and transforming it into an e-book (Stalder, 2021, p. 3). This is a change not only in the presentational nature of the medium (from physical to electronic presence) but also in its quality, usage, and educational consequences: »Other notions characterize Digitality: non-linearity; associative links; parallelism and simultaneity; feedback that merges cause and effect; a thing can be in multiple places at once; each position is always context- and time-dependent, etc.« (Stalder, 2021, p. 4; transl. A.B.) As a consequence, digitalization changes the social appearance of individuals and their knowledge, the opportunities for interaction among participants, and the given medium. Digitalization also opens up various possibilities for connecting, monitoring processes by using their inherent data in time and

---

6   One might refer here to the German use of the term »migration background,« a signifier that marginalizes many people by addressing them as the »others«.

7   For this term see Bolaji's article in this volume.

tracking activities. Thus, compared to physical, analogical media, a very different environment emerges, and very different opportunities and threats in learning and education occur.

This emergence of digitality as a dominant cultural constellation occurred in Germany around the year 2000 (Stalder, 2016, p. 11). It changed the everyday life of individuals (Hauck-Thum & Noller, 2021, p. V) and the possibilities of interaction and labor (Böhmer, 2016).[8]

Through these developments, the need for a new literacy has arisen to enable those involved to become competent citizens of the digitalized world, and to deal with its transformed infrastructure and its educational challenges. These challenges occur from the technical quality of digital media and the new possibilities of presentation, interaction, and evaluation by digitality. Competencies are therefore needed in technical application, methodical usage, understanding of the changing relation between transparency and opacity of behavior, as well as a mindset of usage and acritical attitude regarding digital tools, the settings they offer, and the individual's position in those settings.

Keeping these conceptualizations in mind, we can define *digitality as a paradigm that represents any given thing in a digital form*. More exactly, digitality transfers material and immaterial elements into binary codes, represented in electronic data. Digitality transforms presenting, relating to, interacting with, and the (critical) analyzing of the given elements, such as media, data, or communication, and thus creates a new kind of reality. This has various consequences for learning, education, teaching methodology, and social as well as cultural processes. Digital media, therefore, are never neutral instruments (Krommer, 2021, pp. 57f.), but constitute elements and platforms of a specific environment that challenge learning, and also shape its particular forms and outcomes. Thus, a sense is created (cf. 2.2), but again, in a different form from that conditioned by a non-digital environment (Bettinger, 2022, pp. 9).

Three aspects of digital culture are mentioned regularly in discussions about it: referentiality, communality, and algorithmicity (Stalder, 2021, pp. 5ff.). These terms relate to reference selection, the creation of a common worldview, and algorithmic sorting of perceivables. To these factors, a fourth should be added: mediality. The latter is connected with the other three because mediation is always necessary in order to bridge physical and digital realities. Indeed, not every medium is digital, but every digital presentation needs a »bridge of meaning« into the experienced physical world to function

---

8   This is one of the main goals in the projects this paper refers to; cf. note 1.

there. For example, the digitalized image of physical structures in a navigator's map needs to be transferred into the physical perspective of a driver, so that the user can be led to a targeted destination. The image needs to be »translated« into potential bodily experiences; digitality is related to the *carnal materialization of human existence.*[9] Hence digitality as a core element of modern »Western« culture is associated with the embodiment of the users and their environment; this is an aspect that will require reflection later in more detail.

The temporal aspect of digitality in learning environments should not be overlooked. It is not only the evolution from content management systems (CMS) via learning management systems (LMS) to learning content management systems (LCMS) that has opened the doors for private companies and changed the field of education in recent years (Espejo Villar et al., 2021, p. 114). The COVID-19 pandemic has been a further agency of radical change: »we are witness to a process of ›commercialisation and privatisation of public education through edtech during the emergency of global school closures and home-based learning‹« (ibid., p. 115; citing Williamson & Hogan). Thus, the digitality of learning environments is not only a question of media, infrastructure, and selection processes for the individual. Digitality is also about educational governance that determines a culture of »supply and demand«, and also shapes the possible supply and the experienced demand that are now more intensely pushing in the direction of market-targeted »educational products.« The demand thus arises that »public administrations, as leading agents in a desired democratic educational governance focused on the common good, must assume debates and regulate and control access by these private political agents to the digital education stage.« (Espejo Villar et al., 2021, p. 121)

On the one hand, this intervention seems to be all the more important, as a specific »learning outcome« might be affected by a growing economic perspective in the market-driven educational field: the threat of a curtailment of educational creativity if learning does not relate to creative learning outcomes but only to innovations that are useful for economic markets. On the other hand, with its »massive connectivity and the creation of virtual environments

9   Regarding the »incarnation« of experience in general in Merleau-Ponty (1968). In contrast to his conception of *incarnation*, I here use the term *carnal materialization* to make clear that no mind, perception, imagination, or anything else mental moves *into* the flesh of the body, but that this perception *is* the body itself, and that is the sum total of the material »world« (cf. for further details paragraph 3.1).

with new possibilities for learning« (Henriksen et al., 2021, p. 2093), digitality opens up many opportunities to create new learning results, environments,
and also new triggers and instigating stimuli because of its multi-perspective
and non-linear, associative links (see above).[10] Therefore, new combinations or
findings might occur in digitalized learning settings that allow more creativity. But if learning outcomes are only measured in terms of economic data and
profitability, new outcomes beyond and outside the interests of the economic
sector might be neglected, thwarted, or blocked completely. The reason for this
is that »there are no clear-cut guidelines about how to recognize creativity or
assess its worth, or even to determine who are the appropriate gate-keepers
for its evaluation, or what evaluative measures to use.« (Henriksen et al., 2021,
p. 2103) But as this »transformation« of creativity into economic assets has not
been fully studied or finally researched, it could become a task for critical educational theory to reassert the importance of creativity and (not only econom-
ically assessable) innovation in general, and in digitalized learning environments in particular. Here again, it becomes evident that digitality in learning
environments and its methods are neither neutral nor instrumental, but in a
certain way, political and critical.

   This insight leads to the last aspect of digitality to be discussed: the relevance of embodiment in a digital environment. Many studies refer to »body
gestures, movements and learning« (Xu et al., 2022, p. 1), »based not so much
on symbols and their manipulation, but on perceptual processes and the actions afforded in learning environments« (Johnson-Glenberg et al., 2016, p. 3;
see also Georgiou & Ioannou, 2019; Ioannou & Ioannou, 2020). Digitality and
the embodiment of learners therefore are interconnected, and the significance
of the digital environment for embodied learning is thus not only an addition
to educational practices, but shapes and changes it profoundly. However, the
virtuality of the body in digital learning environments and the consequences
for learning and teaching are seldom in focus (see exceptions in Brinkmann et
al., 2019; to some extent also: Pischetola & Dirckinck-Holmfeld, 2021). This will
be examined here in more detail.

   The reason for this change in educational practices is the relatedness of digitality and the ways of everyday living as well as the results of digital forms of
research (Choi & Chun, 2022, pp. 36f.). Especially those platforms using Augmented Reality offer »embodied experiences shared among users that allow
them to imagine and relive the spatiotemporal depths [...] by actively dwelling

---

10   For the conceptualization of responsive virtuality, cf. footnote 2.

and participating in them« (Choi & Chun, 2022, p. 49). The authors reflect on an example of a historic city and state on which the digital learning platform offers learning material that marks the use of embodied experiences *in* digital learning environments. The above-mentioned navigator's map was another example of connecting digital and physical spaces. Both show that a dichotomy of the physical vs. the digital environment is not plausible, either for navigating bodily relevant structures such as streets, or for the pertinent digital data such as augmented reality. In both cases, the connection between the digital and bodily environment is evident. This leads to the following consideration: digital environments are given in a virtual sense, but bring bodily consequences into the learning process. This is in many ways similar to any physically perceived environment.

Virtuality, however, needs further conceptualization. As classical concepts often follow a dichotomous perspective that distinguishes between bodily and virtual experiences, some recent philosophical approaches point up the entanglement of corporeality and virtuality (Willat & Flores, 2022; but cf. already Merleau-Ponty, 2002, published in 1945). Here, digitality is only »one of the possible modes of the virtual« (Willat & Flores, 2022, p. 34); others, such as olfactory or acoustic, are also possible. Hence, »we should not allow the digital to be the only expression of virtuality that we can experience.« (Ibid.)

Assuming that there is no actual dichotomy between embodied and virtual experiences, but a connection in their *objective* relation to the everyday life of the individual (with its physical and virtual reality) and also in their *subjective* relation to the perception of the individual, learning cannot only be comprehended as a process within the individual and influenced by the environment. Learning within the perspective of interrelated embodied and virtual experiences is in accordance with the structure of the individual, who is embedded within the particular environment and in permanent exchange with it.

In illustration of this position, a statement by Merleau-Ponty might convey further insight: »Truth does not inhabit only the inner man, or more accurately, there is no inner man, man is in the world, and only in the world does he know himself.« (Merleau-Ponty, 2002, p. xii)[11] As this author claims perception and the perceiving subject within its world, this paper follows so far – and marks the relevance of the bodily experience of the subject in its world. Merleau-Ponty defines the embodied presence in the world as follows: »we are – as bodies – fully ›intertwined‹ with the materiality of the world and of others«

---

11   The same certainly applies to every further gender group.

(Vlieghe, 2019, p. 61). Hence, for Merleau-Ponty, the human body and its surrounding world are interwoven and the relationship between them is indissoluble.

This register of perception is not only a physical one (as it is physically given). It can also be a virtual one, as it also operates with the variations of virtuality:

> »For example, the sense of sight is stimulated when we see a cup of coffee on our desk. If we pick up the cup and drink the coffee, other senses such as touch, smell and taste are also stimulated. However, tactile, olfactory or gustatory experiences are not exhausted in what we are actually touching, smelling or tasting, in some way like regular coffee drinkers can already ›touch‹, ›smell‹ or even ›taste‹ the cup of coffee with their gaze and feel the tension it produces in their body, especially when they are sleepy and thirsty. In this case, just looking at the cup arouses virtual movements towards it that may or may not be actualized in concrete actions.« (Willat & Flores, 2022, p. 28)

Thus, virtuality is a bodily function that forms perception itself, and through this also understanding and learning. Virtuality is not opposed to bodily reality but is a part of it. In this view, digitality is not an outcome of technical devices alone, or in the first instance (ibid., p. 22). Rather, it is also a bodily possibility and a form of reality that marks the importance of the bodily presence of the individual, especially when learning in a digital environment: »the experience of the virtual is inherently embodied and fully real« (ibid., p. 23). Following Merleau-Ponty (2002) and the interpretation of Willat & Flores (2022), I argue that the body is a source of »virtuality« in itself and, through this, the co-actor of non-bodily virtuality as given in digital environments. This perspective seems convincing because digital data need to be responded to by the »carnal« individual with the ability to activate virtual practices and de-code virtual elements encountered in the media environment. It is a quality of the body to connect to the environment (called »world« by Merleau-Ponty) and the virtual due to its own »virtuality« and the ability to decode digitality. In other words, different sensory perceptions can be experienced by a single person as interacting with the social or physical environment, e.g. an image activates a particular smell or a theoretical conversation, for instance, in school classes or at university, or stimulates certain other bodily perceptions, further sensations, and answers resulting from them.[12] This means: The »new normal« is not the hybridity of virtual learning – this has been given as long as learning has been a bodily practice – but the digitality of learning as an embodied experience of the single person, embedded into their (learning) environment.

This leads to specific forms of identities. They become more dynamic (Bernal-Guerrero, 2021, p. 15) as the environment they relate to is also dynamic, especially regarding social media (Alonso-Sainz, 2021, p. 54). This »is completely related to the need for otherness that all human beings have to build our identity« (ibid., p. 58). In this view, learning environments are structurally not only cultural but also social. Moreover, as the technological aspects of the digital learning environments develop from the particular cultural settings (Möller et al., 2021, p. 135), they implement these cultural norms and practices – and with them, the social order of the given habitus as embodied culture (Bourdieu, 1984) as well.

To summarize, the aspects reflected in this sub-paragraph can be seen as this: digitality has been a part of Western societies for many years. But it seems that it has not been correctly understood in its bodily aspects, as the body also creates virtuality, and the body's virtuality corresponds with the digitality in the media-technological environment. Hence, to better understand what digitality in learning environments means, one has to reflect on the cultural and social aspects of the embodied individuals taking part, together with the technological elements that import cultural and social norms. Thus, the outcome of digital learning is not only »situated knowledge« (following Haraway, 1988) but also »situated identity«, as far as an embodiment of knowledge and social structure are involved. This can be conceptualized as the »digitalized subjectivation« that occurs in digital learning environments.

3.2 Culture in a Digital Environment

After these more extended reflections on digitality and its cultural characteristics of embodiment, it should have become evident that culture is a concept

---

12   It also seems relevant to note: »it is necessary to examine the spatial-temporal differences that emerge from the media in which corporeal virtuality unfolds. From an analytical point of view, a fundamental difference is to be found between embodied and virtual presence. Whereas the body as an actual physical presence can be here *or* there, the virtual body can be here *and* there.« (Willat & Flores, 2022, p. 32).

of practice, and through this a concept of signification. Culture provides categories describing positions in the field that one can call identities. Culture furthermore provides patterns of interpretation for individuals, groups, and environments. Culture also structures social life and learning contexts. Keeping all this in mind, we can see culture as an instrument of power, subjectivation, positioning, and marginalization in all societies, although particularly in Western ones, especially when it comes to cultural embodiment. Through this, culture is a core path of othering – also in learning environments, as they are social fields for the performance and assessment of embodied learning.

Regarding virtuality, bodily and digital experiences now come into view and show the connection between virtual, digital, social, and cultural aspects. These are not the same. Nevertheless, they interconnect with each other in several ways. This means that neither digital nor virtual media or technical devices are »pure« and neutral. They are always embedded in the given structures and fields, transporting norms, affiliations, positionings, and power endowments.

This is relevant not only for cultural and social relations in general but also for cultural aspects of teaching (cf. paragraph 2.2) and especially for digital teaching, as recent developments during the pandemic have shown (cf. paragraph 3.1).

Some examples will serve to explain this intersection of cultural and social scenarios in digital learning: digital learning environments, for example, provide opportunities to track students' behavior. In a research project on university student-to-student interaction within online learning platforms (Wut et al., 2022), a certain group of students was reluctant to use a discussion forum in Moodle. »They preferred to discuss among their peer group so that they would not lose their ›face.‹ Keeping face is a very important consideration in Chinese people's culture.« (Ibid., p. 8) If there had been reference to »the« culture of »the« Chinese people this would have merited separate discussion in its own right, but it is evident that the cultural practice relevant in this specific course led to specific responses in behavior and thus in learning practices.

But it is not only a question of social practices following a certain cultural normativity. Also, the conditions facilitating digital infrastructure contribute to the formation of the social-cultural intersection of learning practices (ibid., p. 11). »Social influence«, this study found, »is one of the mediators between the Facilitating Conditions and the student-to-student interaction behavior of online learning platforms« (ibid.). Following the paragraph above, this finding explains the specific concept of social behavior in a culturally defined field – and therefore, all three aspects of digital learning need to be kept in mind: social norms, cultural practices, and digital facilities that arrange these practices in allowing or preventing culturally formed social interactions of the students in their bodily performance in the digital environment.

Consequently, digital environments are not only »learning ecologies […] as decentralized self-learning environments which follow varying curatorial principles and agencies involving human and machine entities.« (Möller et al., 2021, p. 132) They also bring about a social-cultural intersection with learning and form it in a particular way. Here again, »situated knowledges« (Haraway, 1988) occur – now not only as epistemological entities but also as social and cultural practices that belong to the given time and place.

To sum up this paragraph: Digitality is a concept of social and cultural practices that opens up different options for learning, interacting, and practicing social relations while generating identities, knowledges, belongings, and exclusions. These generated concepts all relate – in different ways – to the embodied experiences of the learners, also in digital environments. Digital learning platforms thus instantiate the socializing process of individuals learning in a specific environment and lead to culturally structured fields of power. Such aspects of embodiment occur here continually. Therefore, learning in digital environments is not only a question of techniques and methods but, more important, of embodied, social, and cultural identities as well as of the struggle for equity and equality.

Insofar culturality, learning, and social meaning are realized in digital teaching in terms of significations. These significations occur within the particular field, platform, and normativity that refer to the bodies and minds of the learners altogether. What this means will be explained in the next paragraph.

4. Learning as Creation of Social Meaning

So far, it should have become clear that virtuality, digitality, and embodiment interrelate in various forms and thus affect the learning processes in digital environments. Although the question of embodied learning in digital environments has been discussed in several ways, the question of the body as a digital signifier in virtual learning environments needs to be given more attention to calibrate teaching in digital environments. Here, the body is not only understood as an instrument for developing the learner's mind (cf. paragraph 3.1) or a carrier of environmental elements (Medina & Stahl, 2021, p. 206), but as part of the learning environment itself. Following Merleau-Ponty (2002), I emphasize that the body is not distanced from the learning environment or even the opposite of it, but constitutes the learning field together with the social partners and the environment (cf. again paragraph 3.1).

> »All the elements of an environment—student, teacher, interactions, technical objects, climate, place, historical moment, emotions, brain, body, disciplines, events, society, community, relationships, connections—are part of a complex network that characterizes the unique context for learning« (Pischetola & Dirckinck-Holmfeld, 2021, p. 199).

Although the latter authors still espouse the juxtaposition of body and environment by constructing a dichotomy of subject and world (cf. ibid.), they can be agreed with because they list the elements that affect learning – and thus do so also for digital environments. As mentioned above (cf. paragraph 1), learning means signification, understanding, and identification. Signification creates meaning in particular situations and specific cultural and social circumstances that also occur in digital learning environments. Here, signification and decoding happen in a virtual space that differs from the physical in that it is non-linear, associative, parallel, simultaneous, multiply located, and dependent on the context (cf. paragraph 3.1). Thus, new qualities of signification occur. This has consequences for learning as a socio-semiotic concept – for the process and the relation to the content – and needs to be taken account of in the teaching arrangements, for instance in the learning environment. Particularly the body of the learners in their environment is essential (as shown above) as it impacts perception, subjectivation, and (sometimes critical) positioning – not only as physically given but also by emotions, reflections, locomotion, etc. Even more important, perhaps, the body of the learner becomes a digitalized image that shapes the learning process in terms of social differences and cultural discrimination. This has various consequences for the digital teaching of embodied learners, as will be explained immediately.

4.1 The Social Meaning of the Subjectivated Bodies

As shown in the introduction (cf. paragraph 1), signification is meaning-making in addressing, positioning, and subjectivizing individuals and groups. When such signification occurs in digital environments, the specific conditions of the latter need to be considered. The bodily performance is *multi-*

perspective, as it might be seen from various camera angles. However, it is only *two-dimensional* on the screen. It is associated with random individuals in a learning setting and is *parallelized* with all who participate in this digital meeting. It can occur *simultaneously* with that of others (when in synchronous sessions), or *separated* from that of many or even all others (when in asynchronous sessions). This bodily performance can be seen *wherever* learning devices are used. Finally, this bodily performance appears in different ways depending on the given *environmental context*, especially when an avatar is used. But the most relevant aspect this paper intends to bring to the fore is that the embodiment of learning takes place as *part of the environment*, not in opposition to it. This means that a learning environment depends strongly on the participants who use it; a teacher cannot design it alone, but depends on the – visible, audible, etc. – manner in which the learners perform in the digital setting. It is only with the help of factors like this, that the whole learning environment can be created.

This shows the following with regard to digital learning during the pandemic: the pandemic shifted learning settings, bodily performances (in vivo, in digital environments, etc.), social relations and support, and last but not least, the learning arrangements (presence – hybrid – online – blended – inverted – etc.). But what does embodied learning in digital environments mean when the cultural or social framing changes? If it is true that »there is *no meaning without framing*« (Kress, 2010, p. 10), the cultural or social aspects affect the learning environment beyond its digital programming and applications. Once more, it is evident that embodied and technical aspects of the learning environment intersect.

To give an example from my own digital teaching: It makes a difference whether or not students turn their video on and provide insight into their bodily appearance, their bodily behavior, etc. But it also makes a difference whether the students are welcomed with just a general greeting (»Hi everybody! Welcome to today's lecture ...«) or whether they are *hearing* their own individual names so that everybody can feel personally addressed (as could be seen by two of our collaboration partners from abroad when we attended their courses). Hence, the embodied performance, with its bodily addressing, shapes the atmosphere of collaboration and the learning process in the digital environment right from the beginning.

To summarize these suggestions: Ever since the period of the COVID pandemic, the culture of learning has been changing, with perhaps the most significant changes actually taking place during the pandemic period itself.

Not simply the culture, but also the social structure of learning has been profoundly affected. Both factors are related to the learners, their embodied presence in the digital learning environment, and through this their »learning mode«. Learning as embodied reality has changed its settings and thus its culture; therefore the social responses to these changes are also of importance.

4.2 Mind the Social Gap

This leads to the next and final reflection, which focuses on social gaps for learners, especially in digital learning environments. Although one might think that these environments offer everyone the same learning opportunities and potential educational outcomes, various studies show huge differences between the learners, depending on their social status.

Very generally, it is claimed: »There is ample evidence that the pandemic has widened social gaps in societies. Students with restricted housing conditions, limited internet access and poor digital equipment have been impaired by the pandemic more drastically.« (Kerres & Buchner, 2022, p. 4) Recent research on adolescent Germans shows that digital learning during the pandemic troubled many but in different phases of the pandemic and with varying intensities (Andresen et al., 2022, pp. 9ff.). More specifically, these young people most often missed contact with professional counselors (22.9%), emotional support from their families (16.5%), and a person of trust (13.4%) (ibid., p. 11). Those from poorer families feel more depressed (ibid., p. 16). These and many more findings show how social status and social recognition affect the emotional situation of young people and demonstrate how necessary it is for them to be able to participate – in everyday life and learning environments.

On the other hand, digital learning following the pandemic is in academic fields still controversial. As some universities celebrate the »new normal,« others want a »return to normal«. However, neither side is consolidated yet (Kerres & Buchner, 2022, p. 5). The same attitudes can be found among students: »At universities, students might have changed their routines, some have moved their domicile farther away or have picked up a job not easily compatible with fixed appointments in a lecture hall.« (Ibid.). Social gaps also lead to different expectations for the education system and its learning environments. But through this social difference, cultural divergence is also growing: »it becomes all the more important to take digitalization and digital phenomena in educational contexts seriously as structural components in culture, as (not so) new cultural techniques.« (Möller et al., 2021, p. 136) Here, education is both a social challenge and a source of cultural transformation.

Finally, the social and cultural differences need to be considered in their institutional, organizational, and individual aspects, so that the effects of these differences regarding students' identities, learning outcomes, and employment opportunities (Brown et al., 2022, p. 5) can be taken account of. The issue of embodiment for digital teaching in learning environments, therefore, is a multi-layered challenge. It is a challenge of meaning for the individual and their learning processes, issues, and outcomes. It is a challenge for teachers to conceptualize a learning environment that is not only set up for rather different learners but also one constructed together with them and upon their differences. Also, it is a challenge for educational theory and its general reflection on social, cultural, and subjectivated differences that affect the learning processes and, at the same time, change the »world« – to use Merleau-Ponty's term for describing environmental structures the individual is intertwined with. This all means that different meanings occur in situated learning and teaching settings – and create different meanings as a consequence.

4.3 From Social Meaning to Embodied Sense?

This paper has made a very long journey – from questions on socio-semiotic signification (1) via cultural reflection on Western hegemony (2) to digitality as an issue of embodiment to the layers of meaning in digital learning concepts (3). Following Mason's (2014) approach to meaning- and sense-making for understanding basic information or complex contents, we might here ask as to whether the meaning of the digital environments leads to an understanding of »an activity conceived [...] as recognizing and postulating connections or relationships between data and frame« (ibid., p. 209). Bearing in mind the relevance of social and cultural categories and their importance for the signification of embodied identities, it seems plausible that the creation of sense in the digital environment is essential. But the data of a single stage in the learning progression (such as activities on the platform, submission of assignments, etc.) cannot fully explain the progress in learning and the quality of education a learner experiences. Furthermore, the connection between these data and the contextual frame (of the learner, the teacher, the organization, the socio-cultural field, etc.) needs to be considered to better understand the intertwined conception of the embodied learner and the whole framework around them.

In a digital environment, the body is not transparent or even ever the same object that learning refers to. The body is rather both a visible *and* opaque element of the individual and their learning process. This is not only for the physical data concerning the material body but is also the case for the embodied self of the learner as seen by themselves and others, and despite the fact that the learner is still unable to understand every single motion of their bodily presence. Therefore not only the *embodied constitution of the individual* is opaque, but actually also the *individual themselves*.

The core aspect of learning cannot be understood in its completeness and thus may lead to a different form of sense-making. The sense of learning of the opaque individual then is not a finalized concept of instruction and assessment. This version of *opaque learning* is the unforeseeable, situated, and tentative process of understanding the digital field as defined by the reflection of the self that is expressed by the body and, at the same time, challenged by it. So the question remains: are those *digital bodies, learning and teaching*, ever so clear and distinct that their meanings become accessible?

References

Alonso-Sainz, T. (2021). »Don't Be Your Selfie«: The Pedagogical Importance of the Otherness in the Construction of Teenagers' Identity. In: J. M. Muñoz-Rodríguez (Ed.), *Identity in a Hyperconnected Society* (pp. 49–59). Springer International Publishing. https://doi.org/10.1007/978-3-030-85788-2_4

Althusser, L. (2001). Ideology and Ideological State Apparatuses. In: *Lenin and Philosophy and other Essays* (pp. 121–176). Monthly Review Press.

Andresen, S., Lips, A., Rusack, T., Schröer, W., Thomas, S., & Wilmes, J. (2022). *Verpasst? Verschoben? Verunsichert? Junge Menschen gestalten ihre Jugend in der Pandemie.* Universitätsverlag Hildesheim. https://hildok.bsz-bw.de/frontdoor/index/index/docId/1326

Beer, R. & Sievi, Y. (2010). Subjekt oder Subjektivation? Zur Kritik der Subjekttheorie von Andreas Reckwitz. *Österreichische Zeitschrift für Soziologie, 35*(1), 3–19. https://doi.org/10.1007/s11614-010-0043-2

Bernal-Guerrero, A. (2021). Shaping Identities in a Hyperconnected World: Notes for the Refutation of »Pedagogical Levity«. In: J. M. Muñoz-Rodríguez (Ed.), *Identity in a Hyperconnected Society* (pp. 3–13). Springer International Publishing. https://doi.org/10.1007/978-3-030-85788-2_1

Bettinger, P. (Ed.) (2022). *Educational Perspectives on Mediality and Subjectivation: Discourse, Power and Analysis*. Springer International Publishing. https://do i.org/10.1007/978-3-030-84343-4

Böhmer, A. (2016). *Bildung der Arbeitsgesellschaft: Intersektionelle Anmerkungen zur Vergesellschaftung durch Bildungsformate*. transcript. https://doi.org/10.1515/ 9783839434499

Böhmer, A. (2020a). Fremd, nicht immer anders. Zur Bildungsarbeit mit Geflüchteten. In: M.-S. Baader, T. Freytag, & D. Wirth. (Eds.), *Flucht—Bildung—Integration? Bildungspolitische und pädagogische Herausforderungen von Fluchtverhältnissen* (pp. 203–219). Springer VS.

Böhmer, A. (2020b). *Management der Vielfalt: Emanzipation und Effizienz in sozial-wirtschaftlichen Organisationen*. Springer Fachmedien. https://doi.org/10.10 07/978-3-658-25372-1

Böhmer, A., Isso, I., Schwab, G., & Sahin, H. (2022). Blended Learning Mobility: Konzepte, Erfahrungen, Perspektiven aus dem Projekt »Digital and International Virtual Academic Cooperation« (DIVA). *Ludwigsburger Beiträge zur Medienpädagogik, 22*, 1–13. https://doi.org/10.21240/lbzm/22/21

Bourdieu, P. (1984). *Distinction: A Social Critique of the Judgement of Taste*. Routledge.

Bourdieu, P. (1986). The Forms of Capital. In: J. Richardson (Ed.) & R. Nice (Transl.), *Handbook of Theory and Research for the Sociology of Education* (pp. 241–258). Greenwood.

Bourdieu, P. & Passeron, J.-C. (1990). *Reproduction in Education, Society and Culture* (2nd Ed.). SAGE Publications Ltd.

Brinkmann, M., Türstig, J., & Weber-Spanknebel, M. (Eds.) (2019). *Leib – Leiblichkeit – Embodiment: Pädagogische Perspektiven auf eine Phänomenologie des Leibes* (Vol. 8). Springer Fachmedien Wiesbaden. https://doi.org/10.1007/ 978-3-658-25517-6

Brown, N., Zipf, S., Pagoto, S., Waring, M. E., Hatfield, N., Palmer, L., Lewis, K. A., & Workman, D. (2022). Emergency remote instruction in 2020: Differential impacts on science, technology, engineering, and mathematics students' confidence and belonging, by gender, race/ethnicity, and socioeconomic status. *Frontiers in Education, 7*, 915789. https://doi.org/10.3389/fedu c.2022.915789

Brubaker, R. (2004). *Ethnicity Without Groups*. Harvard University Press.

Butler, J. (1992). Contingent Foundations: Feminism and the Question of »Postmodernism«. In: J. Butler & J. W. Scott (Eds.), *Feminists Theorize the Political* (pp. 3–21). Routledge.

Chen, B., Håklev, S., & Rosé, C. P. (2021). Collaborative Learning at Scale. In: U. Cress, C. Rosé, A. F. Wise, & J. Oshima (Eds.), *International Handbook of Computer-Supported Collaborative Learning* (pp. 163–181). Springer International Publishing. https://doi.org/10.1007/978-3-030-65291-3_9

Choi, J. E. & Chun, J. (2022). Toward an integrated digital humanities: A deep reading. *International Journal of Digital Humanities, 3*(1–3), 35–50. https://doi.org/10.1007/s42803-021-00035-2

Davis, H. (2004). *Understanding Stuart Hall*. SAGE Publications Ltd.

Derrida, J. (1982). *Positions* (A. Bass, Ed.). University of Chicago Press. https://press.uchicago.edu/ucp/books/book/chicago/P/bo24847338.html

Espejo Villar, L. B., Lázaro Herrero, L., Álvarez López, G., & García Gutiérrez, J. (2021). Collaborative Digital Governance: Pseudo-Educational Identities on the International Political Agenda? In: J. M. Muñoz-Rodríguez (Ed.), *Identity in a Hyperconnected Society* (pp. 109–123). Springer International Publishing. https://doi.org/10.1007/978-3-030-85788-2_8

Foucault, M. (1988). An Aesthetics of Existence. In: L. D. Kritzman (Ed.), *Politics, Philosophy, Culture. Interviews and Other Writings, 1977–1984* (pp. 47–53). Routledge.

Georgiou, Y. & Ioannou, A. (2019). Embodied Learning in a Digital World: A Systematic Review of Empirical Research in K-12 Education. In: P. Díaz, A. Ioannou, K. K. Bhagat, & J. M. Spector (Eds.), *Learning in a Digital World* (pp. 155–177). Springer Singapore. https://doi.org/10.1007/978-981-13-8265-9_8

Haase, C., Povolná, R., & Schmied, J. (2007). Complexity and Coherence – Outlining a Mosaic. In: C. Haase, R. Povolná, & J. Schmied (Eds.), *Complexity and Coherence: Approaches to Linguistic Research and Language Teaching* (pp. 1–12). Cuvillier Verlag.

Hall, S. (1982). The rediscovery of »ideology«; return of the repressed in media studies. In: M. Gurevitch, T. Bennett, J. Curran, & J. Woollacott (Eds.), *Culture, society and the media* (pp. 52–86). Routledge.

Hall, S. (1996). The West and the Rest: Discourse and Power [1992]. In: S. Hall, D. Held, D. Hubert, & K. Thompson (Eds.), *Modernity. An Introduction to Modern Societies* (pp. 184–224). Blackwell Publishers.

Hall, S. (1997). Old and New Identities, Old and New Ethnicities. In: A. D. King (Ed.), *Culture, Globalization, and the World-System: Contemporary Conditions for the Representation of Identity* (pp. 41–68). University of Minnesota Press.

Haraway, D. (1988). Situated Knowledges: The Science Question in Feminism and the Privilege of Partial Perspective. *Feminist Studies*, 14(3), 575–599. https://doi.org/10.2307/3178066

Hauck-Thum, U. & Noller, J. (Eds.) (2021). *Was ist Digitalität? Philosophische und pädagogische Perspektiven*. J.B. Metzler. https://doi.org/10.1007/978-3-662-62989-5

Henriksen, D., Creely, E., Henderson, M., & Mishra, P. (2021). Creativity and technology in teaching and learning: A literature review of the uneasy space of implementation. *Educational Technology Research and Development*, 69(4), 2091–2108. https://doi.org/10.1007/s11423-020-09912-z

Ioannou, M. & Ioannou, A. (2020). Technology-enhanced Embodied Learning. *Educational Technology & Society*, 23(3), 81–94.

Johnson-Glenberg, M. C., Megowan-Romanowicz, C., Birchfield, D. A., & Savio-Ramos, C. (2016). Effects of Embodied Learning and Digital Platform on the Retention of Physics Content: Centripetal Force. *Frontiers in Psychology*, 7. https://doi.org/10.3389/fpsyg.2016.01819

Kerres, M. & Buchner, J. (2022). Education after the Pandemic: What We Have (Not) Learned about Learning. *Education Sciences*, 12(5), 315. https://doi.org/10.3390/educsci12050315

Kress, G. (2010). *Multimodality. A social semiotic approach to Contemporary communication*. Routledge.

Krommer, A. (2021). Mediale Paradigmen, palliative Didaktik und die Kultur der Digitalität. In: U. Hauck-Thum & J. Noller (Eds.), *Was ist Digitalität? Philosophische und pädagogische Perspektiven* (pp. 57–72). J.B. Metzler. https://doi.org/10.1007/978-3-662-62989-5_5

Kruse, M.-M. (2022). *Politik, Medien und Jugend*. transcript.

Laclau, E. (2006). *Emancipation(s)*. Verso Books.

Laclau, E. & Mouffe, C. (2013). *Hegemony and Socialist Strategy: Towards a Radical Democratic Politics*. Verso Books.

Lave, J. & Wenger, E. (1991). *Situated learning: Legitimate peripheral participation*. Cambridge University Press.

Lehmann-Rommel, R. (2015). Unterrichtsgespräche aus semiotisch – pragmatistischer Perspektive. In: H. de Boer & M. Bonanati (Eds.), *Gespräche über Lernen—Lernen im Gespräch* (pp. 61–82). Springer Fachmedien. https://doi.org/10.1007/978-3-658-09696-0_4

Magnusson, P. & Godhe, A.-L. (2019). Multimodality in Language Education – Implications for Teaching. *Designs for Learning*, 11(1), Art. 1. https://doi.org/10.16993/dfl.127

Mason, J. (2014). »Does it Make Sense« or »What Does it Mean«? In: C.-C. Liu, H. Ogata, S. C. Kong, & A. Kashihara (Eds.), *Proceedings of the 22nd International Conference on Computers in Education, ICCE 2014* (pp. 206–211). Asia-Pacific Society for Computers in Education.

Medina, R. & Stahl, G. (2021). Analysis of Group Practices. In: U. Cress, C. Rosé, A. F. Wise, & J. Oshima (Eds.), *International Handbook of Computer-Supported Collaborative Learning* (pp. 199–218). Springer International Publishing. https://doi.org/10.1007/978-3-030-65291-3_11

Merleau-Ponty, M. (1968). *The Visible and the Invisible, Followed by Working Notes*. Northwestern University Press.

Merleau-Ponty, M. (2002). *Phenomenology of Perception*. Routledge.

Möller, E., Unterberg, L., & Jörissen, B. (2021). Cultural Sustainability and (Post-)digital Transformation(s) in the Context of Aesthetic, Arts, and Cultural Education. In: B. Bolden & N. Jeanneret (Eds.), *Visions of Sustainability for Arts Education* (Vol. 3, pp. 125–139). Springer Singapore. https://doi.org/10.1007/978-981-16-6174-7_12

Pischetola, M. & Dirckinck-Holmfeld, L. (2021). Exploring Enactivism as a Networked Learning Paradigm for the Use of Digital Learning Platforms. In: N. B. Dohn, J. J. Hansen, S. B. Hansen, T. Ryberg, & M. de Laat (Eds.), *Conceptualizing and Innovating Education and Work with Networked Learning* (pp. 189–210). Springer International Publishing. https://doi.org/10.1007/978-3-030-85241-2_11

Posselt, G. & Flatscher, M. (2018). *Sprachphilosophie: Eine Einführung*. utb.

Saussure, F. de. (1989). *Cours de linguistique générale*. Otto Harrassowitz Verlag.

Scherr, A. (2012). Cultural Studies. In: U. Bauer, U. H. Bittlingmayer, & A. Scherr (Eds.), *Handbuch Bildungs- und Erziehungssoziologie* (pp. 319–334). VS Verlag für Sozialwissenschaften. https://doi.org/10.1007/978-3-531-18944-4_20

Stalder, F. (2016). *Kultur der Digitalität*. Suhrkamp Verlag.

Stalder, F. (2021). Was ist Digitalität? In: U. Hauck-Thum & J. Noller (Eds.), *Was ist Digitalität? Philosophische und pädagogische Perspektiven* (pp. 3–7). J.B. Metzler. https://doi.org/10.1007/978-3-662-62989-5_1

Vlieghe, J. (2019). Being-Entirely-Flesh. Taking the Body Beyond its Merleau-Pontian Confines in Educational Theory. In: M. Brinkmann, J. Türstig, & M. Weber-Spanknebel (Eds.), *Leib – Leiblichkeit – Embodiment* (Vol. 8, pp. 57–75). Springer Fachmedien Wiesbaden. https://doi.org/10.1007/978-3-658-25517-6_4

Waldenfels, B. (1994). *Antwortregister*. Suhrkamp Verlag.

Waldenfels, B. (2022). Globalität, Lokalität, Digitalität: Herausforderungen der Phänomenologie. Suhrkamp Verlag.

Willat, C. & Flores, L. M. (2022). The Presence of the Body in Digital Education: A Phenomenological Approach to Embodied Experience. *Studies in Philosophy and Education*, 41, 21–37.

Wut, T. M., Lee, S. W., & Xu, J. (Bill). (2022). How do Facilitating Conditions Influence Student-to-Student Interaction within an Online Learning Platform? A New Typology of the Serial Mediation Model. *Education Sciences*, 12(5), 337. https://doi.org/10.3390/educsci12050337

Xu, X., Kang, J., & Yan, L. (2022). Understanding embodied immersion in technology-enabled embodied learning environments. *Journal of Computer Assisted Learning*, 38(1), 103–119. https://doi.org/10.1111/jcal.12594

Empirical Findings

Inter- and Transcultural Experience among Future Foreign Language Educators
International Virtual Exchange between Teacher Training Institutions

Beverley Topaz, Tina Waldman, & Götz Schwab

1. Introduction

It might sound surprising, but the pandemic did not affect us to a great extent, at least not regarding the way we teach and collaborate within our transnational framework. What we report on in this chapter dates back to 2015, when we decided to collaborate online in what today is usually called virtual exchange, heron VE, and thus laid the foundation of the experience in the DIVA project reported here. Of course, we had limited experience with such formats at the beginning of our partnerships, as only one of the authors had participated in an online collaborative project before (Waldman & Harel, 2015). Nonetheless, over the course of the years, we were able to improve and further develop our skills and knowledge – technically, pedagogically and interculturally – so that the cooperation during the pandemic turned out to be the most rewarding and intense online collaboration between our two in-stitutions so far. Before reporting on the DIVA collaboration between the two English departments of Kibbutzim College of Education, Technology and the Arts in Tel Aviv, Israel, and Ludwigsburg University of Education, Germany, we provide an overview of the most important aspects of how VE in foreign language teacher training is characterised. Following the description of our programme, insights into our research findings are given, where the main focus is on the students' perspective and experience. In our conclusion, we suggest how online collaborations can be conducted successfully in a post-Covid era.

2. Virtual Exchange and Foreign Language Teacher Training

Virtual Exchange (VE), Collaborative Online International Learning (COIL), or Telecollaboration are terms used almost interchangeably in the literature (e.g. Belz, 2003; Dooley, 2008; Helm, 2016; O'Dowd, 2007, 2018). In this chapter we use the term VE and define it in the following way:

VE supports the idea of online communication via digital tools to bring together language learners in geographically remote places. It fosters language and intercultural competences through collaborative tasks and/or project work. It is rooted in Task-Based Language Teaching (TBLT) and Project-Based Language Teaching.

(PBLT) respectively. Most importantly, this approach is student centred, and knowledge and understanding are constructed through student-to-student interaction.

In this description, several important aspects are highlighted: international collaboration, digital literacy, language learning, language teaching methodologies, and inter- and trans-cultural learning (Schwab & Drixler, 2020). A primary pedagogical goal of VE is to foster intercultural communicative competence (ICC), intercultural learning and critical cultural awareness (Avgousti, 2018; O'Dowd, 2011). VE was originally limited to universities in the 1990s (Warschauer, 1996) and moved into teacher education some decades later (O'Dowd, 2015). Today VE also takes place on a growing scale between schools and school children in diverse areas of the globe (Papadakis, 2016).

VE has its roots in international remote collaboration and student email exchange. However, this idea can be traced back to scholars such as Célestin Freinet or even Jardine (Dooley, 2007) who encouraged their students to send letters to students in other countries. With the emergence of the World Wide Web and the rapid development of the internet, more projects were launched and supported by essential stakeholders in the field of education (EU, government ministries, school boards, etc.) (Baroni et al., 2019). Today there are various models of VE, and generally teachers design their model according to their pedagogical goals and the resources available (O'Dowd, 2018). This involves teacher partners working closely both at the stage of design and throughout the collaboration to facilitate the entire process and to deal with unexpected issues as they arise.

The collaborations described in this chapter were part of a project funded by the German Association of Academic Exchange (DAAD). This chapter deals with one of two parts of the overarching DIVA programme and focuses on the collaboration between prospective English language teachers in Israel and Germany.

3. Description of the collaborations

The collaboration described here consists of two parts which differ in respect to student cohorts, the main focus of collaborations and their time frames. However, both parts were developed, planned and conducted in close coordination. On the Israeli side, two facilitators (the first two authors) were involved, whereas on the German side, both collaborations, conducted in two consecutive semesters, were facilitated by the same person (the third author).

3.1 DIVA – the first steps: Undergraduate collaboration

The first leg of our DIVA contribution, taught in the summer of 2021, is part of the undergraduate study programme of both colleges and comprises a VE where students experience intensive online exchange with other students from different cultures. This VE was initially designed and facilitated by two facilitators (authors two and three) from the respective institutions in Israel and Germany (Waldman, Harel, & Schwab, 2016). One of the major goals of the collaboration is to establish relations among participants by providing an intercultural learning experience based on constructivist principles (Sadler & Dooly, 2016; O'Dowd, 2015). The first VE took place in the fall semester of 2015 between two classes of third year undergraduate pre-service teachers of English as a foreign language (EFL). The students met online weekly for about 45 minutes throughout the semester and collaborated on tasks and a final project based in their separate institutions. This VE, which has now become institutionalised, has taken place every fall over the last seven successive years with different student cohorts numbering over 300 participants so far (Schwab & Drixler, 2020).

The course programme has undergone a number of changes since its inception, with the facilitators building on research studies, reviewing regular student feedback, and integrating current digital tools, as well as making adjustments to meet students' needs, which were especially pressing during the Covid pandemic when students were forced to study from home. The semester-long process was as follows: each course began with an information exchange between students. Prior to the first meeting, the students posted a short introduction about themselves on Flipgrid (a video recording platform). The students viewed each other's openings so that they could recognize each other during their first synchronous meeting, which consisted of a video conference discussion where they talked about issues such as student life, their respective institutions and educational systems in their countries, as well as what motivated them to choose a career in teaching.

The second stage of information exchange supported the team formation process. Students were divided by the course facilitators into teams comprising two or three partners from each country. In a team video conference (via Zoom), students discussed similarities and differences regarding cultural practices prompted by discussions around images of cultural artefacts that they had posted on Padlet before the meeting. Based on this exchange, they discovered a common foundation across cultures and developed a team name, working philosophy, and rules of conduct for their interaction (see also Baroni et al., 2019). This provided a common bond to support them in the continuing process while working together. It soon became obvious that by this stage, with online contact and communication between team members in and outside the classroom, close bonds had formed, which were essential prerequisites for collaborating successfully on a final digital product (Byram et al,2002). Together, team members analysed teaching materials focusing on intercultural learning tasks and decided on a list of fundamental criteria for developing culturally sensitive learning materials. They used these criteria to design their product: learning materials and communication tasks employing several multi-modal contexts through the integration of various digital platforms. Before finalizing, the products were uploaded to the shared Moodle Platform for peer review and revision. The last session of the course included a video conference, in which the students voted for the best products according to pre-established criteria.

Finally, the last stage involved the students writing reflective essays documenting their personal experiences and what they had learned throughout the course. Throughout the VE the facilitators employed different strategies to support the students in meaningful communication, as well as in delicate issues that sometimes arose between team members. One such method involved the facilitators creating a task that urged the participants to tackle cultural differences which students tend to steer away from in what seems to be an effort to avoid confrontation. As facilitators, we ensured that communication during this task could take place safely, and if discomfort arose, we provided explicit mentoring to the students involved. Over the course of the collaboration, we, the facilitators, stayed in permanent contact with each other via mail and regular video conferences.

3.2 DIVA – The next step: graduate collaboration

As a result of the successful collaboration between the undergraduate students described above, we embarked [GS1] on a new VE programme designed for Post Graduate Students of Education in Kibbutzim College of Education and M.A. students in Ludwigsburg University of Education, all of whom were studying to become EFL teachers (Böhmer, Schwab, Isso, forthcoming).

The collaboration began in the fall of 2021 during the Covid-19 pandemic when students in both countries were studying online. The rationale behind this collaboration was to examine the impact of Covid-19 on EFL methodologies and practices in the two countries. An additional objective was – and thus in line with the first course – to increase students' cultural awareness and intercultural competences, as well as to provide a model for students on the implementation of VE within their own classes.

Students also met weekly for approximately 45 mins on Zoom, though only for four consecutive weeks, due to our individual course constraints. Before the first session, students were required to pinpoint where they were located in the world using Padlet. They were also asked to upload an artefact, i.e. a picture of an object, which represented their personal identity. In breakout rooms comprising mixed groups of 2–3 participants from both institutions, students shared information about their geographical location and discussed the artefacts they had chosen to upload. Towards the end of the first session, all reconvened in the main room to share insights they had gained from the activities.

The second session focused on their professional identities as EFL teachers and educators. The Padlet platform was once more used to facilitate this discussion, which was held in the same mixed groups that had been formed previously.

In the third session, students were asked to share their perceptions of the challenges and opportunities that the pandemic had afforded them as (future) teachers. To facilitate this process, they were directed to a shared google drive document in which they discussed and documented what they would like to »keep in their suitcases« and what they would like to »pack away in their closed suitcases«. The suitcase analogy was used to exemplify new tools and methods they believed they had acquired and to enable them to rethink practices they believed were no longer effective or appropriate. The assignment for the next session was to decide as groups how they would present a framework for teaching EFL in the post-pandemic era, including statements on their teaching philosophy and concrete suggestions for the English language classroom.

In the fourth and final session, also done via Zoom, students were given time to work on their frameworks for teaching EFL and to present them briefly to their peers, as the allotted time would not allow an intensive discussion. This was done in a written reflection similar to what we had conducted in the first leg of our DIVA online cooperation with the undergraduate students.

Although this online collaboration was more confined in its time frame and workload, it did not seem to be less intensive for either students or facilitators. This might be because the cohort of students was more mature, especially on the Israeli side, where all students were older, as they had all embarked-on teaching as a second career. It might also be due to the fact that the limited amount of time encouraged students right from the beginning to be more focused. It is worth mentioning that this collaboration was conducted during a military campaign in Israel. Israeli students were subjected to air-raid sirens, and many had spent time during the night and during the online sessions in bomb shelters. This might have contributed to increased expressions of empathy on the part of the students in Germany. The Israeli students had been given the option to drop out of the collaboration, yet all chose to remain in the group. This might have been because they had been in lockdown for an extended period and were craving social interaction with others, albeit via zoom.

4. Research

Although a major part of the DIVA project was to provide participants with the opportunity to meet students from different cultures and backgrounds, we also integrated a research perspective into our endeavours from the start.

4.1 Methodology

The study is a mixed method study, which uses varied methods of data collection to capture different dimensions of the effect of the collaboration on participants. Three data sets were collected from the Israeli and German students: written reflections based on guiding questions, Zoom break-out room video recordings and collaborative online-products created by the transnational teams. In this chapter, we will focus on the written reflections. By writing the guided reflections, participants were encouraged to share their insights on their experience, their perceptions of knowledge and skills gained, as well as the nature of the interaction with their overseas partners, and their perceptions of intercultural awareness and competence. Both sets of reflection essays were analysed using thematic analysis methodology (Braun & Clarke, 2006) and the emerging themes of (1) digital literacy, (2) intercultural awareness and learning (3) collaboration and (4) Continuing Professional Development (CPD) were identified. The products showcased participants' knowledge and application of skills acquired during the collaboration (for more details see also our project websites: www.telecollaboration.eu and www.diva-project.de)

To avoid ethical complications, the researchers followed the Ethical Standards of the American Educational Research Association (AERA, 2011) regarding confidentiality, integrity and informed consent. All participants were assured that participation or lack of it in the study would not interfere with their assessment or grade for the course.

4.2 Written reflections

Due to the differences in the nature of the two courses, the guiding questions for the written reflections differed to some extent. In the undergraduate course, we underscored the role of language and intercultural learning, whereas, for the graduate course, we put more emphasis on teaching methods and pedagogical knowledge. Nonetheless, both cohorts reflected on the use of digital tools and mobile devices in teaching (foreign) languages and dealt extensively with the notion of inter- and transcultural competences. In the following sections, we will exemplify our categories with several sample quotes from the written reflections of both cohorts (n=81[1]).

4.2.1 Digital Literacy
Digital literacy is not just »a key factor in enabling participation in education« (Martin & Grudziecki, 2006, p. 249) but also a »broad concept, linking together other relevant literacies, based on computer/ICT competences and skills, but focused on ›softer‹ skills of information evaluation and knowledge assembly, together with a set of understandings and attitudes« (Bawden 2008, p. 28). It

---

1   I.e. undergraduate cohort: 27+20 German/Israeli essays, cohort 2: 21+13 German/Israeli essays. However in the second cohort, some Israeli students opted for a joint document.

encompasses other literacies, such as information or media literacy and emphasises its usage in social online spaces (Lankshear & Knobel, 2008). In this vein, the notion of digital online learning and development of digital literacy can certainly be considered as being at the heart of VE and Telecollaboration. Nonetheless, we could not take it for granted that digital competences and digital literacy develop automatically.

We, therefore, incorporated the use of digital tools in various ways to promote digital literacy. Students were encouraged to try out a wide range of tools and, at the same time, were given the opportunity to discover, implement and experience new platforms whenever possible and meaningful. Students appreciated this across the board:

> »We think the use of digital tools in this collaboration was excellent and is necessary first and foremost as a way of helping us communicate and getting our creative juices flowing.« (Israeli, graduate)

Interestingly, most of the technological input was provided by fellow students, often from their international partners who introduced new digital tools to the collaboration.

> »I wrote down all the tools that both my group and the other groups used in their product and will use them later.« (German, undergraduate)

Another interesting aspect which arose from the written reflections was the difference in the use of technology in the two countries; this was evident in the following statement:

> »The LUE students were really surprised and impressed that we have a projector in every classroom in Israel and that it is used daily in many lessons. This led to an interesting discussion regarding digital tools, which they rarely use and therefore are less acquainted with them.« (Israeli, graduate)

As digital tools are not an end in themselves, a significant goal of the project was to focus on The critical use of digital tools to serve pedagogical aims in teaching languages to students of various ages and levels – also an essential aspect of digital literacy among future teachers:

»We were taught that technology is important and knowing how to use a specific technological tool that suits a specific assignment is an amazing way to engage students.« (Israeli, undergraduate)

Students developed a critical stance on digitalisation and the use of mobile and digital devices by reflecting upon their use in the language classroom.

»These and more tools I gratefully put into my teaching toolbox. Of course, however, one should always be critical and not see digital interaction as a panacea. Every tool must continue to be critically scrutinised and tested.« (German, graduate)

Such a reflective stance towards digitalization is an important aspect of digital literacy and can help to empower participants in becoming competent members of their own »community of learning« (Martin & Grudziecki, 2006, p. 258), be it in a national or international context.

4.2.2 Intercultural awareness and learning

One of the main objectives of these collaborations was to increase students' intercultural sensitivity and awareness in order for them to better understand intercultural differences, to avoid and reflect upon stereotyping and to develop a curiosity about others (Byram et al., 2002). We were interested in examining to what extent we had achieved this aim. Looking at the following reflections, it seems as if we reached at least some of our goals:

»I have definitely extended my intercultural skills during this online collaboration. I think I have developed the intercultural skill to never judge a different culture by how they act or react. I have extended my ability to understand different cultural contexts and viewpoints, and moreover my acceptance to different cultural settings.« (German, undergraduate)

and

»Because the many cultures out there are so diverse, it is difficult to prepare them specifically for each one. However, working closely with people of even one other culture allows students to transfer these experiences to other such encounters through competencies like multiperspectivity, tolerance and open-mindedness.« (German, graduate)

Nevertheless, this quote reveals that some students are still unaware that even in ›one‹ culture, there are students from diverse backgrounds.

Furthermore, not all participants managed to develop this sensitivity and remained entrenched in their prior stereotypes, apparently unable to transcend them.

> »To be truly honest, what I anticipated was exactly what I experienced. I knew there would be a behavioural difference.« (Israeli, undergraduate)

External conditions, specifically the military campaign in Israel that occurred during the collaboration with the second cohort, did, however, create an opportunity for increased intercultural sensitivity and empathy. This was evident in the written reflections of both German and Israeli students:

> »I admit, my first thoughts of cultural awareness were like traditions, special foods or housing situations. But never in my life would I have thought of missile attacks and war!« (German, graduate)

> »We did not talk about politics at all, but during the zoom meeting that took place during the military campaign, they were very empathetic. Both girls were interested in what was happening, wanted to hear first-hand information and told us how the media in Germany was very biased. It was important to them to hear how we felt and they could not digest the fact that rockets were being sent towards our homes to harm us.« (Israeli, graduate)

Nevertheless, as is evident in the following reflection, some students realised that to become culturally competent, more than one such transnational experience is required.

> »We know that global learning is inherently cumulative and multifaceted, and therefore difficult to cover through a single experience, but despite that this one-time experience has contributed a lot.« (Israeli, graduate)

Due to unexpected current events, namely the above-mentioned military campaign in Israel, the facilitators decided to concentrate less on their prepared and predesigned lesson plans. They deemed it more important to afford the students the opportunity to get to know each other and allow for time to express their feelings and fears resulting from the precarious security situation. Students recognised and appreciated this change in plan.

> »The current events were also the reasons why we were not able to discuss all the tasks and issues that needed to be resolved. We thought it was more important to give them the time to talk about their experiences and how they feel about them.« (German, graduate)

or

> »My cultural awareness was increased as I was able to communicate with people that live under different circumstances. This helped me to sympathise and engage in topics that I only know through the media.« (German, graduate)

These reflections emphasise the need for facilitators of VE to be flexible in their lesson plans and to be willing to ›go with the flow‹ and address the needs of the learners. Additionally, intercultural experience can only be planned to a certain degree. Planning also depends on the context of the collaboration and sometimes there are unpredictable circumstances beyond the control of the facilitator.

4.2.3 Collaboration

One of the potential pitfalls in facilitating VE is ensuring the effective collaboration amongst students from diverse backgrounds, with differences in teaching experience, disparate levels of language mastery in English and varying degrees of motivation, as becomes evident in the following statement:

> »The difficulty of working effectively was less due to us being encultured differently, but rather due to having different motivations, language skills, knowledge about language teaching, didactics, etc.« (German, undergraduate)

Nevertheless, the role of the facilitators and the meticulous design of the tasks can make a marked difference to the attainment of the goals of the collaboration:

> »In my point of view, the whole process described went so smoothly because of the way we were introduced to each other in the beginning. I think the

two artefact-tasks were perfect considering the fact that we had something to talk and ask about.« (German, graduate)

The importance of providing carefully structured tasks to promote effective discussion was appreciated by the participants. Nevertheless, some felt that not enough effort had been made on the part of the facilitators to provide more detailed instructions and to better match the prior experience of the students from both countries and programs.

> »In terms of the process around group work, we thought it could maybe have benefited from more instructions, expectations, or recommendations from the professors. There could have also been a way to match types/levels of experience people on both sides have.« (Israeli, graduate)

On the whole, though, the participants enjoyed the opportunity to collaborate on their joint projects, which related to both education and culture.

> »Interacting with the German students on such important topics such as culture and education was refreshing and interesting.« (Israeli, undergraduate)

In addition, students recognised that despite the geographical and cultural differences, they also have much in common:

> »[...] we are very similar; both as students and future teachers, we have the same challenges, concerns, and experiences. These differences sparked interesting conversations about the various aspects of being a teacher – our studies, salaries, status, and more.« (Israeli, graduate)

The Israeli students were envious of the high status the teaching profession enjoys in Germany, in stark contrast to the low status the profession has at present in Israel, a fact that might affect one's identity as a teacher.

4.2.4 Continuing Professional Development (CPD)

Another pedagogical goal of our project was to encourage students to examine their professional identities as well as to model for them more inclusive pedagogical strategies and current pedagogical methods to assist them in addressing the challenges of increasingly diverse classrooms. According to Mann & Webb (2022, 14–15) CPD is a process and therefore »ongoing in its efforts to promote professional learning and standards, and it fosters innovation, collaboration, and reflection«. The DIVA project targeted these three dimensions of professional development.

It seems evident from the students' reflections that they understood that the formation of a professional identity as an educator and teacher is something that evolves and transforms over time:

>But what I could take away the most from the collaboration, and what is the most important for me, is that I could learn from my partners that it takes a long time to find your professional identity.« (German, graduate)

All participants expressed the desire to attempt to incorporate principles modelled in the collaboration into their own classrooms in the future:

>I will definitely take this experience and I will try to place it somehow into my future classroom.« (German, undergraduate)

or

>The collaboration has made clear to me how important thinking outside our box and therefore outside our comfort zone is.« (German, graduate)

One student was explicit about the teaching technique she would implement.

>One example of applying what I have experienced in this course to my teaching is to use the opportunity of letting the students teach each other things they specialise in, without me explicitly teaching them that.« (Israeli, undergraduate)

Students related as well to the pedagogical principles implemented in the VE and stated that they would incorporate these principles into the practice of their future professions as English language teachers:

>Requiring students to comment on others' posts encourages them to practise writing in English and being empathetic. In addition, the collaboration required us to use different skills such as writing, speaking, listening, critical thinking, and more ... All these skills, steps, and tools will be in mind when conducting such a collaboration in the future.« (Israeli, graduate)

The reflections revealed that many students started to develop a sense of what characterises the notion of CPD, that is, a critical and reflective attitude towards one's teaching behaviour that can be described as »a long-term process […] that teachers learn over time« (Oesterle & Schwab, 2022, p. 46). Our project is a step in this direction and encourages students to process situations and ideas that are hardly addressed in regular study programmes.

4.3 Conclusion and looking ahead

Our experiences have shown that VE has the potential to increase pre-service teachers' intercultural competences to a certain degree. It became evident in their reflections that awareness towards cultural similarities and differences was present, and that they displayed curiosity and empathy towards each other. This behaviour was particularly salient during the military campaign in Israel in 2021 when team members in Germany expressed concern for and kindness towards their Israeli counterparts.

These findings are limited as we have only included self-reported written reflections in this part of our study. Nonetheless, the findings are in line with those of many other scholars in the field (e.g. Dooley, 2008; Guth & Helm, 2010; Guth, Helm, & O'Dowd, 2012; O'Dowd, 2018; 2021; Sadler & Dooly, 2016; Schenker 2010) and therefore contribute to a better understanding of VE and its potential. We believe that these intercultural competencies are essential for educators planning to teach successfully in their communities and abroad. All classrooms today consist of learners from diverse cultural backgrounds and the ability to be sensitive to these differences is crucial for all educators. Pre-service teachers studying to teach EFL seem to be a particularly suitable target population for carrying out such collaborations, as English can in these circumstances serve as a neutral language where issues of language mastery are not involved (Waldman, Harel, & Schwab, 2019). Usually, participants are not mother tongue speakers of English, thus eliminating issues of control and language hegemony.

If carefully designed, collaborations as described in this chapter have the potential to model for students current pedagogical principles, including the critical use of digital tools and up-to-date language pedagogy, thereby contributing to students' repertoire of techniques and strategies to be used in their future classrooms (Baroni, 2019; O'Dowd, 2021). Ironically, it appears that the Covid-19 lockdowns, which forced Higher Education Institutions to transfer all their teaching to online platforms, contributed to the success of our collaborations. This is due to students' digital infrastructure and WIFI-connection being more reliable from home than from campus, making collaboration easier for us as teacher educators and VE facilitators.

Moreover, enforced government lockdowns imposed during the pandemic appeared to heighten the need and desire for interaction with others, albeit only online. Meeting regularly during this period to collaborate online seemed to enhance student motivation. However, now that students have returned to face-to-face learning they may perhaps be experiencing ›Zoom fatigue‹ (Nesher Shoshan & Wehrt, 2022) and be less enthusiastic to participate in VE. This would require facilitators to rethink their planning for future collaborations, and e.g. extend VE with study abroad opportunities (Topaz & Waldman, 2022). One model could be the Extended Telecollaboration Practice (ETP) model that we introduced elsewhere (Waldman, Harel, Schwab, 2019) and which underscores the importance of combining VE with physical exchange – short periods of study abroad where students collaborate both in person as well as online. O'Dowd (2018, p. 20) stated, »[t]he future of virtual exchange appears to be bright yet still unclear in many respects«; we could add that its brightness depends on the flexibility and openness of the participating facilitators and stakeholders towards new and sometimes unforeseeable technological, pedagogical, social and even historical developments.

References

American Educational Research Association (2011). Code of ethics, *Educational researcher*, 40(3), 145–156.

Avgousti, M.I. (2018). Intercultural communicative competence and online exchanges: a systematic review, *Computer Assisted Language Learning*, DOI: 10.1080/09588221.2018.1455713

Baroni, A., Dooly, M., García, P. G., Guth, S., Hauck, M., Helm, F., Lewis, T., Mueller-Hartmann, A., O'Dowd, R., Rienties, B., Rogaten, J., & Rogaten, J. (2019). *Evaluating the impact of virtual exchange on initial teacher education: A European policy experiment*. Research-publishing. net.

Braun, V. & Clarke, V. (2006). Using Thematic Analysis in Psychology, *Qualitative Research in Psychology*, 3(2), 77–101.

Byram, M., Gribkova, B., & Starkey, H. (2002). *Developing the Intercultural Dimension in Language Teaching: a practical introduction for teachers. Language Pol-*

icy Division, Directorate of School, Out-of-School and Higher Education, Council of Europe.

Böhmer, A., Schwab, G., & Isso, I. (2023). Blended Academic Communication. On technology-Enhanced Teaching and Learning in Digital and International Virtual Academic Cooperation (DIVA). In: J.S. Stephen, G. Kormpas, & C. Coombe (Eds.), *Global Perspectives in Higher Education: From Crisis to Opportunity* (pp. 129-143). Springer. https://doi.org/10.1007/978-3-031-31646-3 _10.

Böhmer, A., Isso, I., Schwab, G., & Sahin, H. (2022). Blended Learning Mobility –Konzepte, Erfahrungen, Perspektiven aus dem Projekt »Digital and International Virtual Academic Cooperation« (DIVA). In: T. Knaus, T. Junge, & O. Merz (Eds.), *Lehren aus der Lehre in Zeiten von Corona. Mediendidaktische Impulse für Schulen und Hochschulen* (pp. 149–161). Kopaed.

Bowden, D. (2008). Origins and Concepts of Digital Literacy. In: *New literacies: Concepts, Policies and Practices* (pp. 17–32). Peter Lang.

Council for Higher Education (2018). *Policies for Promoting Digital Learning.* CHE, Israel. [Hebrew] [Google Scholar]

Dooly, M. (Ed.) (2008). *Telecollaborative Language Learning: A Guidebook to Moderating Intercultural Collaboration Online.* Peter Lang.

Guth, S. & Helm, F. (Eds.) (2010). *Telecollaboration 2.0: Language, literacies and intercultural learning in the 21st century* (Vol. 1). Peter Lang.

Guth, S., Helm, F., & O'Dowd, R. (2012). *University language classes collaborating online. A report on the integration of telecollaborative networks in European universities.* https://www.unicollaboration.org/wp-content/uploads/2016/06/1.1-Telecollaboration_report_Executive_summary-Oct2012_0.pdf

Lankshear, C. & Knobel, M. (2008). *New literacies: Concepts, Policies and Practices.* Peter Lang.

Mann, S. & Walsh, S. (2017). *Reflective practice in English language teaching* (1st Ed.). Routledge. https://doi.org/10.4324/9781315733395-1

Mann, S. & Webb, K. (2022). Continuing professional development: key themes in supporting the development of professional practice. In: G. Schwab, M. Oesterle, & A. Whelan (Eds.), *Promoting professionalism, innovation and transnational collaboration: a new approach to foreign language teacher education* (pp. 15–44). Research-publishing.net. https://doi.org/10.14705/rpnet.2022.57.1382

Martin, A. & Grudziecki, J. (2006). *DigEuLit: Concepts and Tools for Digital Literacy Development, Innovation in Teaching and Learning in Information and Computer Sciences*, 5(4), 249–267, DOI: 10.11120/ital.2006.05040249

Nesher Shoshan, H. & Wehrt, W. (2022). Understanding »Zoom fatigue«: a mixed-method approach. *Applied Psychology, 71*(3), 827–852.

O'Dowd, R. (2011). Intercultural communicative competence through telecollaboration. *The Routledge handbook of language and intercultural communication* (pp. 340–356). Routledge.

O'Dowd, R. (2015). »Supporting in-service language educators in learning to telecollaborate«, *Language learning and technology, 19*(1), 63–82.

O'Dowd, R. (2018). From telecollaboration to virtual exchange: State-of-the-art and the role of UNICollaboration in moving forward. *Research-publishing. net, 1,* 1–23.

O'Dowd, R. (2021). What do students learn in virtual exchange? A qualitative content analysis of learning outcomes across multiple exchanges. *International Journal of Educational Research, 109,* 101804.

Oesterle, M. & Schwab, G. (2022). Developing a framework of CPD for the context of foreign language teaching. In: G. Schwab, M. Oesterle, & A. Whelan (Eds.), *Promoting professionalism, innovation and transnational collaboration: a new approach to foreign language teacher education* (pp. 45–79). Research-publishing.net. https://doi.org/10.14705/rpnet.2022.57.1383

Papadakis, S. (2016). Creativity and innovation in European education. Ten years eTwinning. Past, present and the future. *International Journal of Technology Enhanced Learning, 8*(3–4), 279–296.

Sadler, R. & Dooly, M. (2016). Twelve years of telecollaboration: what we have learnt. *ELT journal 70*(4), 401–413.

Schenker, T. (2012). Intercultural competence and cultural learning through telecollaboration. *CALICO Journal, 29*(3), 449–470. https://doi.org/10.11139 / cj.29.3.449-470

Schwab, G. & Drixler, N. (2020). Telekollaboration und Digitalisierung in der Hochschullehre: Interkulturelles Lernen durch virtuellen Austausch im Studium zukünftiger Lehrerinnen und Lehrer. In: D. Elsner, H. Niesen, & B. Viebrock (Eds.), *Hochschullehre digital gestalten in der (fremd-)sprachlichen LehrerInnenbildung. Inhalte, Methoden und Aufgaben* (pp. 235–254). Narr Francke Attempto Verlag.

Topaz, B. & Waldman, T. (2022). Internationalization for Nurturing Intercultural Communicative Competencies in Pre-Service Teachers (pp. 203–215). In: Yitzhaki, D., Gallagher, T., Aloni, N., & Gross, Z. (Eds.), *Activist Pedagogy and Shared Education in Divided Societies: International Perspectives and Next Practices.* BRILL.

Waldman, T., Schwab, G., & Harel, E. (2019). Extended Telecollaboration Practice (ETP) in Teacher Education: Towards Pluricultural and Plurilingual Proficiency. *European Journal of Language Policy/ Revue européenne de politique linguistique, on the subject of Languages and international virtual exchange (special edition)*. *11*(2), pp. 167–185.

Waldman, T. & Harel, E. (2018). Promoting online collaboration competence among pre-service English as Foreign Language (EFL) Teachers. *Collaborative learning in a global world*. Literacy, Language and Learning series. Information Age Publishing.

Waldman, T. & Harel, E. (2015). Participating in a technology enhanced internationalization project to promote students' foreign language motivation. In: D. Schwarzer (Ed.), *Internationalizing teacher education: successes and challenges within domestic and International contexts*. Lexington Books.

Waldman, T., Schwab, G., & Harel, E. (2016). Getting their feet wet: trainee EFL teachers in Germany and Israel collaborate online to promote their telecollaboration competence through experiential learning. In: S. Jager, M. Kurek, & B. O'Rourke (Eds.), *New directions in telecollaborative research and practice: selected papers from the second conference on telecollaboration in higher education* (pp. 179–184). Research-publishing.net. [https://research-publishing.net/display_article.php?doi=10.14705/rpnet.2016.telecollab2016.505]

Personal Interlocution in Telecollaboration
Cultural Discourse Analysis of a German-Israeli Virtual Exchange among future EFL teachers

Svenja Meier

1. Introduction

Over the last decades and especially through the COVID-19 pandemic, digital collaborations and networking have become a very important aspect of everyday life; even in teaching and learning digitalization cannot be excluded. Nevertheless, teachers from different parts of the world still hardly exchange their expertise with one and another, even if learning about different cultures and beliefs are parts of the intercultural communicative competence which is an essential constituent in many curriculums (Kilian, 2016; Byram, 1997)

Through projects, such as the DAAD[1]-funded program Digital and International Virtual Academic Cooperation (DIVA) from 2021, students have the opportunity to interact with other student teachers and cooperate in telecollaborative projects.

In previous German-Israeli virtual exchanges conducted in the last few years (Waldman, Harel, & Schwab, 2016, 2019), the students engaged in personal conversations which were not necessarily part of the given assignments and therefore the question arose how and in which form individuals display their personal narratives and beliefs in these digital meetings. This article will take a phenomenological approach to analyze an excerpt of one recorded session between a group of German and Israeli students who participated in the DIVA project in the winter term of 2020/2021. The analysis will be an example of an individual narrative and how it is presented in the discourse. Similar

---

1   DAAD stands for *Deutscher Akademischer Austauschdienst*, i.e. the German Academic Exchange Service.

to Salonen's (2018) study, the focus will lie on the self-disclosure represented in the interlocutors' dialogue with an intention on language use. Further, the multimodal observations will be discussed on the basis of Carbaugh's (2007) cultural discourse analysis (CuDA). Findings and areas for discussion will be linked to the theoretical background of CuDA and narrative inquiries which are fundamental components of expression and performance of an individual. I will place my conclusions on the findings of the presented extract in the conclusion.

2. Theoretical Background

Cultural Discourse Analysis

In the last decades globalization has not only formed economy and technology, but also education which calls for transformation in schooling and teachers to adapt to a rapidly changing landscape of mobility and migration (Savva, 2017). These changes also evoke the need for discourse analysis to include the more culturally diverse constituents and take into consideration that intercultural communication plays an essential role in the understanding of effective communication with appropriate awareness and pragmatics across cultural differences (Byram, Gribkova & Starkey, 2002; Byram, 1997, 2009).

These expectations can be met by an interpretive stance, such as the *Cultural Discourse Analysis (CuDA)*, a concept coined by Carbaugh (2007). The author defines communication as a practice which goes hand in hand with culture and includes: 1. How is communication shaped as a cultural process? and 2. What system of symbolic meanings or what culturally commentary is imminent in practices of communication? Therefore, Carbaugh questions how one presents one's (a) *being*, namely own personhood, explicitly and implicitly as well as the (b) *relationships* that are presumed and engaged between the individuals. Further, he states that (c) how one acts (*acting*) and (d) expresses their *feelings* in communication, displays their cultural background and stand which is shaped by the (e) place and environment of one's upbringing and living, specifically their *dwelling*. The following extract, which was taken from one of the meetings between students discussed here, will demonstrate the ideas of Carbaugh's five principles:

Conversation Extract 1

```
I3: no like ((looking up)) uhm in tel aviv it´s okay
    but we have jaffa, you know, jaffa is uhm next to
    tel  aviv  ((clapping  her  hands  together,  S2
    nodding)) is like in tel aviv. and jaffa all these
    years  we  live  okay arabs  and  eh  jews  together
    NEIGHbors. but no:w (.) uhm in the streets also in
    jaffa and also in akko and it it´s near the sea
    uh they´re friends ((moving her| head towards the
    screen)) there arabs and jews and no:w ((looking
    to the left)) they´re like uhm
    (---)
G3: =divided?
I3: everything is FIRE (,) fire on the street and
```

This conversation, between a German (G3) and an Israeli (I3) student, took place whilst Israel was being threatened by bombs and missiles (and the Israeli counter attacks towards the Gaza strip) during the Israeli-Palestinian conflict in May 2021. It demonstrates how the listener can understand that I3 is an Israeli student living in Tel Aviv and growing up in a society where neighbors recently began fighting each other. Further, G3 is following along in the conversation and is the listener which leads back to the relationship both have. I3 also tells something about her feelings in the way she is describing the shootings as »fire«. In addition, her gestures, such as looking up whilst talking or clapping her hands, also present her form of acting. Even though this is only a small extract of a longer conversation, it gives the reader a lot of information about the cultural background, when following Carbaugh's CuDA.

For that reason, the chosen data of narratives will be discussed on the base of Cultural Discourse Analysis which takes the aspects of »being, relating, acting, feeling and dwelling« (Carbaugh, 2007, p. 174) into account.

Narratives & Personal Interlocutions

Various disciplines and corresponding definitions make it difficult to narrow down the concept of identity. The term identity is often used when describing someone's character und behavior, based on their home culture, surrounding and upbringing (Gee, 2015; Butler, 2006). In the field of TESOL and Applied Linguistics scholars assume that everyone has multiple identities and that these identities change depending on context and time (e.g. Butler, 2006; Gee, 2015; Norton, 2000). Norton (2000) for example states that SLA theorists have not yet been able to define a convincing concept of identity that includes the language learner and the context in which language learning takes place. Nevertheless, there is a growing interest in researching identity construction of teachers in the classroom (Li Li, 2020; Chinokul, 2021). For the course of this article a brief overview and localization of the term *identity* is needed to understand the importance and use of narratives in the digital age.

Teachers' identity is often a combination of their professional and personal identity (Salinas & Ayala, 2017). According to Salinas and Ayala (2017), personal components, such as the individual biography, gender, age and culture are used to shape a teacher's identity. Further, influential components are emotions and language. Taking scholars like Vygotsky (1978) into consideration, language is an important part of identity construction, since identity can be narrated through language, besides language helps in understanding a person. Other scholars, such as Kleinke, Hernández & Bös (2018), divide identity into three parts: personal, group and collective. Whereas the first is the »bundle of traits that we believe makes us unique« (Polletta & Jasper, 2001, p. 298) and the second refers to the membership of an individual in a group, such as class or gender. The concept of collective identity is represented through similar beliefs and knowledge but is also, as well as group identity, defined by macro-categories, such as political affiliation or ethnicity (Kleinke, Hernández & Bös, 2018). For authors, such as Butler (2006) and Baumann (2000) identity is presented in performance. Baumann (2000) for example describes how the individual needs a performative act for individualization:

> [...] ›individualization‹ consists of transforming human ›identity‹ from a ›given‹ into a ›task‹ and charging the actors with the responsibility for performing that task and for the consequences (also the side-effects) of their performance (Baumann, 2000, p. 31–32).

Depending on the research perspective, different components are relevant in defining identity. From a linguistic and language learning perspective, the use of language and the discourse in which language is used, is the desirable focus. In line with Salinas and Ayala (2017) citation that »stories are conceived to express and construct identity through discourse« (Salinas & Ayala, 2017, p. 36), this article will use *self-disclosure* as a way to understand the concept of personal identities expressed in discourse. Self-disclosure is defined as the »process of revealing personal information relating to oneself« (Salonen, 2018, p. 58). An indicator for investigating these examples is the use of self-reference, such as I-statements, e.g. »I think it's something for me that that came with age« or »we in Germany believe that students need to learn at least one foreign language in school«.

For more than thirty years, researchers use stories and narratives as an essential part of investigation (see for example Clandinin et al., 2007; Amott, 2018, 2021) and a growing number of such research has focused on student teachers and teacher novices. Studies, such as the case study conducted by Salinas and Ayala (2018), in which they explored how EFL teachers formed their identity throughout their teaching program, share the interest in using narratives in student teacher research. They concluded that teachers' identity construction is »complex, and teachers must negotiate and reshape their identities through social interactions and experiences« (Salinas & Ayala, 2018, p. 45). Chinokul (2021) mentions that the »knowledge of self is seen as an essential aspect for being a teacher« (p. 430) and that in the process of becoming a teacher »teacher identity—what beginning teachers believe about teaching and learning as self-as-teacher—is of vital concern to teacher education« (Bullough, 1997 as cited in Salinas & Ayala, 2018, 34). Further, Richards (2006) points out that there is also a »default« (p. 60) identity which is presented in the context of discourse and therefore relevant in teacher-student interactions, since these are dependent on the expectations that derive from a classroom setting. In this context, the teacher is the one asking questions, guiding the students in their learning process, imparting knowledge, whereas the student is the person who is answering the given questions, receiving learning advice and knowledge.

Qualitative research, especially narrative inquiries, has explored how teachers articulate their self »through talk, social interaction, and self presentation« (Zembylas, 2003, p. 215) in situated contexts, such as the classroom. By taking a performative view of narrative discourse, »it is in [the] narrative that we construct identities« (Benwell & Stokoe, 2006). Besides, Benwell and Stokoe state that »[n]arrative theorists claim that lives are made coherent and meaningful through the ›biographical‹ work that people do« (p. 130). For this reason, narratives can be used to voice the understanding of self which is visible in one's performance. However, these stories then need to be viewed under two aspects which were defined by Amott (2021, p. 3) as:

(1) socially constructed and therefore nuanced according to the audience and
(2) multiple, meaning that a person might construct their identities differently for different audiences and purposes.

Another component which is relevant for the purpose of this study is the digital age and the individual performance in online settings. Being online does not only determine everyone's life, but there is also a constant fluid switch between being online and offline as well as having private or public conversations. Baumann (2000), who did not refer to internet communication, states that

> [t]he disintegration of the social network, the falling apart of effective agencies of collective action is often noted with a good deal of anxiety and bewailed as the unanticipated ›side effect‹ of the new lightness and fluidity of the increasingly mobile, slippery, shifty, evasive and fugitive power. But social disintegration is as much a condition as it is the outcome of the new technique of power, using disengagement and the art of escape as its major tools (p. 14).

According to him »liquid modernity« (Baumann, 2000) leads to the »loss of stability and certainty as to who we can be and what we can do and say« (Iedermann & Caldas-Coulthard, 2008 as cited in Kleinke, Hernández & Bös, 2018, p. 2), making it a challenge to determine oneself in relation to others in the physical and digital world.

For the purpose of this paper the concept of personal narratives was not explicitly chosen when data was collected, yet it has turned-out to provide meaningful access to the data since it gives insights into the individuals' experiences which then can be used to draw a conclusion of their understanding of culture and language. The following representation of the data collection and methodology will serve as a framework for the analysis and discussion.

3. Data & Methodology

The data was collected in the summer semester 2021 and was part of the DIVA project which was conducted with the University of Education, Ludwigsburg (Germany) and the Kibbutzim College of Education, Technology and the Arts in Tel Aviv (Israel) as well as the Charles Darwin University in Darwin (Australia), however, the latter was not considered in the following data. 43 teacher students, 10 males and 33 females, participated in the project. There is an age difference between the students from Israel and Germany, because the German students are still in their master (age 21 to 27) and the Israeli students all have work experience which is now extended through a teaching degree. Over a period of four weeks the students worked together in synchronous Zoom meetings and discussed pedagogical relevant take-aways from the COVID-19 era. Their findings were collected in digital presentations, such as Microsoft PowerPoint.

In the first two sessions the students got to know each other through Padlets. The first Padlet, which was used in the initial session, was a map of Germany and Israel with set pins to show the others where each group member was from. Students then talked about the surrounding area and recognized things they knew about the other country. The second activity, which was also used in the first meeting, was a personal artifact which the students had uploaded to the Padlet prior to the meeting. The given instruction was to bring an artifact that represents the student's personal identity. Students engaged with each other about the different artifacts of their group members and found similarities, for example in hobbies or interests or they expressed their dislikes. At the end of the session all students met with their professors in the main meeting room and reported back their experience in the group and received the assignment to upload a professional artifact, which represented their teaching personality, to a third Padlet and also to explain why they chose this artifact. This Padlet was the content of the second session. Some students used visuals which included pictures from students or teaching materials, whereas others chose personal artifacts that influence their teaching professionality. After the group session, the students shared their thoughts on things that surprised them or discussed which differences they recognized in their professional identities.

For this paper a video sequence (0:09:17-0:14:26) from the second meeting was selected and transcribed in TRANSANA according to the GAT 2 conventions (Selting et al., 1998). The sequence was chosen because of the way in which the interlocutors communicated and not communicated with each other. The data was then coded in MAXQDA.

The six teacher students, three Israelis (female) and three Germans (one male and two females), uploaded their teaching/professional artifact ahead of time in a Padlet and then took turns in presenting and talking about their choice. These »ice breakers« then partially led to extended, sometimes even controversial discussions.

4. Data Analysis

Padlet Artifact 1

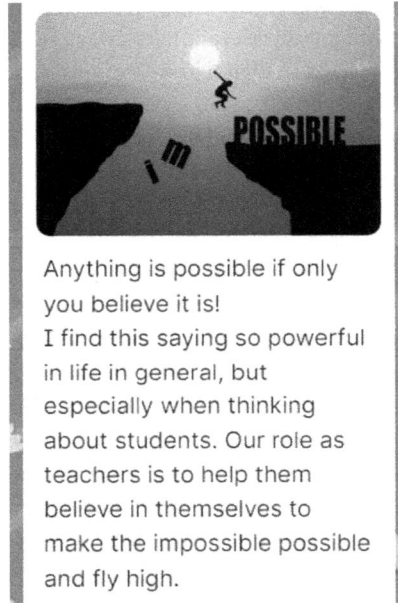

Anything is possible if only
you believe it is!
I find this saying so powerful
in life in general, but
especially when thinking
about students. Our role as
teachers is to help them
believe in themselves to
make the impossible possible
and fly high.

The analyzed sequence is predominantly a monologue of one Israeli student (I2) whose artifact is a picture of herself as a yoga teacher. Prior, another Israeli student (I1) talks about passing on the belief of things being possible: »anything is possible if you believe it is« which is her interpretation of the photography of someone who is jumping over a cliff (Padlet Artifact 1) with the letters »impossible« falling apart. She explains that this is a maxim which refers to every part in life and not necessarily only to teaching.

Her mentioning of the principle initializes the conversation about believing and making things in life possible which then leads to the following sequences.

Conversation Extract 2

```
80    I2:   (--) do you do you guys mind if i go next
            cause it´s
81          kind of to do with this as well
82    G1:   yeah that´s okay
83    G2:   go ahead
84    I2:   o mine i´m just gonna go up it´s just a little bit
85          up for me i just wrote- where is it uh it´s on the
86          right wait(.)
87    I3:   this is a beautiful picture
88    I2:   thanks yeah this was a proper photography with light-
89          ing and make-up
90    I1:   [oh
91    I2:   [just i don´t wake up like this
92    I1:   ((laughs))
```

I2 asks the others if she is allowed to go next, since her artifact and the corresponding explanation is linked to the prior presentation. Everyone agrees and her presentation begins with a focus on her picture and the others complementing her (line 88). Further, I2 states that »[she doesn't] wake up like this« (line 91) and I1's laughs. I2 demonstrates that she has humor and by I1's laughing she connects with her on the level of relationship. Using compliments or humor can be a way of building a relationship between the interlocutors.

In line 96, I1 links back to her own presentation about things being »(im)possible« (as shown in the picture above) by stating that I1 made it possible when screensharing the Padlet, so that everyone can see her picture. This is another form of showing the relationship between I2 and I1 and it also is a compliment for I2 and acknowledging her efforts.

Conversation Extract 3

```
93    I2:   can you guys see it [though
94    I1:                       [we see it see it´s possible ((laughs))
95    I2:   [it's possible
96    I1:   [you made it possible ((laughs))
97    I2:   exactly totally possible uh wait i'm gonna take it up take
98          it up for me it´s just your you guys your [camera
99    I3:                                             [is that you o.
100   I2:   yeah it is
```

The conversation then leads into I2's monologue in which she talks about herself being a yoga teacher and that she practices meditation. She says that she »sees« the difference between times in which she practices meditation and in which she does not. In spite of that, I2 does not interact directly with the other interlocutors, nor wait for their reactions, she continues talking and presenting herself by linking one thought to the next like an ongoing thread. This form of disclosure tells the others that this is an important part of her life:

Conversation Extract 4

```
105   I2:   [...]get's down to the to the real basis of a lot of
106         the fears and i think that when we take that away and
107         i obviously i don't mean fear of like uh let's do
108         something dangerous nothing will ever happen to me
109         i'm not scared not that kind of fear cause that's a
110         good fear uhm but i think it's really all about
111         narratives and it's a lot of the stories you tell
112         yourself and and for me practicing meditation really
113         helps me to get in touch with the essence of myself
114         which is always a loving being and i think that of
115         all humans, yeah it's not just me and and that's very
116         helpful to
```

She also expresses her feelings about fears and how her performance as yoga teacher helps her cope and deal with the essence of life and herself and how this affects her place in society and interacting with others. The way in which I2 keeps the connection to the other interlocutors and upholds the relationship, is by relating back to I1's earlier statement without actively engaging the others in the conversation (line 116) and by looking into the camera whilst speaking. I2 picks up the topic of things being »(im)possible« and says that nothing is impossible. She reinforces her belief by sharing her personal experience of her not being able to get pregnant. For her being pregnant was not possible and a struggle with many negative emotions, such as anger, disappointment and heartache in the last years (line 117–119). However, she now has found a way to have a baby through surrogacy (line 120) which is possible in Israel, but illegal in Germany. This chance has changed her attitude to positive emotions, such as happiness (line 125–126). However, I2 also admits that surrogacy caused fear of what others might think of her (line 122–123). I2 reveals something about her self at this point because she points out that she cares about what others think of her.

Conversation Extract 5

```
116    I2:        [...] to uhm to me and i wanted to say also about
117               what k. what k. uh said that nothing is
118               impossible's that i've been trying to get pregnant
119               for four years and after four years and a lot of
120               disappointment a lot of heartache a lot of tears
121               a lot of anger like so much bad stuff we made the
122               decision to try surrogacy and it's working and
123               she's week twenty-three and i'm so happy and there
124               was so much fear so much fear of what will people
125               say and how will it look to the outside and i'm
126               just so happy that even though i was scared i
127               still did it because i really like think that it's
128               mainly in the head cause everyone's, like so happy
129               for me nobody [cares
130    I1:                      [its in their head
131    I2:                              [people said to me you're an insp
132               ration which it thought was hilarious because i
133               was thinking what will people say i didn't i would
134               be an inspiration and so uhm
```

I1 tries to finish I2's sentence and adds »it's mainly in the head« (line 128), though, I2 ignores the interruption and continues with her story. By stating »people said to me you're an inspiration which i thought was hilarious because i was thinking what will people say i didn't i would be an inspiration«. I2 demonstrates how her personal situation of a surrogacy also hides the fact that she is insecure and unsure about what others might think. This intimacy is an example of showing »feelings« (Carbaugh, 2007).

I2 keeps the floor in the conversation and is still presenting her artifact through screen sharing. Yet the others engage and demonstrate relationship and their feelings towards I2 through gesture and mimicry, such as nodding as an act of affirmation or as described in the following:

Screenshot of Group Meeting

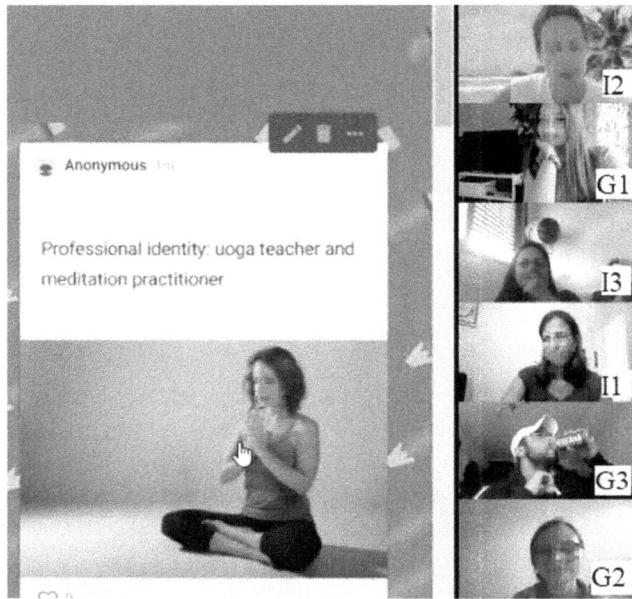

While I2 is talking about her surrogacy, one German student is smiling (G1) and the two other Israeli students (I1 & I3) are nodding their heads. Yet, the male student, who is from Germany, (G3) does not seem to be participating in the conversation because he takes his can to drink something and therefore does not seem to show any form of empathy. G3's behavior is also a good example of avoiding to show feelings as it is an intimate female topic which he may not be able to cope with openly. This behavior may suggest that his »dwelling« is different and so he cannot relate to what I2 is saying. On the one hand, G3's reaction could be because he is not interested in the topic, maybe due to his gender or age. On the other hand, the term »surrogacy« is a very specific terminology which may not be part of his vocabulary and consequently he does not react because he simply does not understand the term or even asks about it. I2 then picks up on the fact that there is an age difference between the Israeli and the German students which makes the two female Germans smile:

Conversation Extract 6

```
134    I2:      i know you guys are still young so it
135             maybe sounds weird to you but if you're
136             an older woman it's really tough sometimes so and
137             also just when you can't when you try to get
138             pregnant and you can't it's such a miserable
139             experience because you think wow what's wrong with
140             me and and the truth is that it just sometimes
141             happens i'm not the first woman it's happened to
142             i mean it's i mean it should theoretically go(es)
143             quite easy but for some women it doesn't anyway
144             my point is that i'm so happy that i thought out
145             of the box and i let go of trying to fight it and
146             i just let go and it worked out {hopefully
```

I1 wants to show her sympathy (line 147–152) and tries to pick up the conversation by giving her opinion. However, I2 interrupts her with »but« (line 153) which gives the impression that she does not agree with I1. I2 wants to make clear that she was afraid of what others would think about her (line 154) and even worse if others would feel sorry for her and her situation (line 159). I1 tries to understand her (line 160), but I2 still feels the need to emphasize that she does not want to come across as someone who is weak and who has problems (line 161–163). It seems as if I2 feels satisfaction of bringing her message across when I1 says »this is just noise« (line 168–169), meaning that I2 does not have to listen to others and even repeats herself to make this point clear.

Conversation Extract 7

```
147    I1:      [amazing amazing i think it's about what
148             you focus on you focused when you focused on
149             what people would say what would they think this
150             is not the main and the most important thing to
151             focus on this is just a side we need to focus on
152             the essence like you said [so
153    I2:                              [but i think that that
154             the uhm the what will people say thing for me
155             i'm sure i'm sure other people too but it's like
156             you realize when you really look into yourself
157             it's such a big thing because it it's not uh
158             like (--) on of things i was scared about is
159             that people would feel sorry for [me
160    I1:                                      [mhm
161    I2:                                      [that's what i
162             mean it's not what will people say like oh she
163             did so and [so
164    I1:                [mhm
165    I2:                [it's that they would be like ohh
166             poor woman i would be so embarrassed [to be in
167             that situation
168    I1:                                          [this is
169             just noise
170    I2:                                          [yeah
171    I1:                                          [this is
172             noise that you have [to
```

The conversation takes a new direction when I3 participates as well. She is also from Israel and shares the same story (line 173). This directly builds a connection between the two which is followed by emotions and verbalizing verbs of action (»No way, I'm crying«, line 175) and even codeswitching into their mother tongue Hebrew (line 179 and 183).

Conversation Extract 8

```
173    I3:    [o. i also i also did this uh my son is now six
174           years old
175    I2:    no way i´m [crying
176    I3:                [so i´ll talk to you [later
177    I2:                                     [oh my god
178    I1:    amazing
179    I2:    (speaks Hebrew)((laughs))
180    I3:    yeah yeah, so we´ll talk
181    I2:    i just wanna| say the waiting is insane
182    I3:    insane
183    I2:    (speaks Hebrew)
184    I3:    so good luck ((giggles))
185    I2:    thank you
186    I1:    i´m so happy for you
187    I3:    ((giggles))
188    I2:    thank you wow
189    I3:    ((laughs))
```

The conversation suddenly becomes very personal and emotional, without including the other interlocutors. Both even decide to follow up with their conversation at a later point (»so i'll talk to you later« and »so we'll talk«) (line 176). Since I3 knows what I2 is going through, she repeats the feeling that the waiting is »insane« (line 181–182). She also wishes her »good luck« (line 184). I1 tries to participate in the conversation then by expressing how happy she is (line 178 and 186), I3 just giggles as a response whereas I2 thanks her (line 185). It is interesting that the whole conversation only takes part between the three Israeli students and is mainly led by I2.

In the following discussion the article will lead back to the two initial questions posed by Carbaugh (2002) and the concept of the CuDA.

5. Findings & Discussion

In this section the findings demonstrated above in the analysis will be discussed by relating back to the five principles: being, relating, acting, feeling, and dwelling. Since the focus is on the interlocutor talking about her surrogacy and how nothing is impossible, the main focus of the discussion will lay on her as an example of personal interlocution.

being

The interlocutor I2 starts with a short description about herself, her social identity, meaning one position in society, (»I'm a yoga teacher and I also practice meditation«). Even though this meeting is about professional identity, she lays her focus on these two personal aspects. The question is: what characteristics come along with someone who identifies themselves as a yoga teacher? She describes practicing meditation as being able to come to the basics of her fears and also focusing on herself. Moreover, she sees herself as a loving being which she thinks of all people. Further she believes that nothing is impossible and explicitly says that she is happy since she has been trying to get pregnant and had the courage to try surrogacy. Implicitly she also expresses who she is by not letting anyone else interfere or interrupt her presentation. In addition, she turns compliments into humor, for example when I3 compliments her picture and I2 then says: »just don't wake up like this«.

relating

As stated above the question about relationships and relating to one another in discourse is also a question as to how relationships are presumed and engaged in communication practices (Carbaugh, 2002). Throughout the extract some forms of relating are explicit, for example when I2 is linking back to I1's statement or when I1 agrees with I2 by saying »exactly its in their head«. I1 also shows agreement with »like you said«. Another explicit form of relating is presented when I3 tells I2 that she has also experienced surrogacy and both interlocutors talk about their experience. There are also implicit actions of proving relation, such as using compliments. One example is when I1 tells I2 that it is »amazing« for her that I2 is fighting for letting go and experiencing this form of becoming a mother (line 147–152). Another example is when I2 shows her emotions »no way, I'm crying« (line 175), after A says that her son who came from a surrogate mother is now six years old.

acting

The principle of acting refers to things that are done whilst talking and these are then explicitly explained (see also Baumann, 2000 on performance). One example can be found at the beginning of the chosen discourse when I2 is looking for her picture in the Padlet and she comments her search: »where is it «p> uh it's up on the right wait« (line 85). I2 also comments the placement of the camera and how she needs to change it so that she can see everyone (»uh wait i'm gonna take it up take it up for me it's just your you guys your camera«, line 98–99). However, since this is an online session, not much action can be seen explicitly.

feeling

As stated above, interacting in the online world changes the perspective of how we present ourselves and how intimate we may get in conversations. According to Carbaugh (2002), the principle »feeling« also includes questioning what affection is appropriate and to which degree.

Talking about not being able to get pregnant and the chance of surrogacy, which is legally not possible in Germany, shows how personal a cross-cultural conversation, especially in an online setting, may get. Furthermore, not demonstrating actions or taking part in a conversation also leads to conclusions of someone's stance towards a topic, for example that none of the German students is actively engaging in the conversation. Nevertheless, not everyone shares this insight and approach, especially when the personal environment is different. This can be seen in how the female German students do not respond to the conversation and only smile when I2 talks about it. It could even be that their knowledge of language does not include the term »surrogacy« because this is not part of their daily life and experience. Further, the way the male student is reacting to the conversation also demonstrates some form of affect because he does not seem to participate at all at this point, but looks the other way or even drinks, whilst others are actively listening. This may not only be a cultural issue, but also linked to the gender differences.

dwelling

People from different cultures and places in the world have a different sense of their environment and where they are located. Depending on the topic this can be an issue for the interlocutors. However, in the analyzed example the inter-locutors do not explicitly refer to their place or environment. This is only done implicitly through the conversation about surrogacy which is, as stated before, not possible in Germany. It is interesting to see that the German students do not engage in further discourse at this point, nor is there any explanation or room for the others, since the conversation's emphasis is on the dwelling of the Israelis only.

This section demonstrated how the theoretical concepts of CuDA were taken to understand the personal interlocutions in an exemplary sequence. A conclusion will be drawn in the following section.

6. Conclusion

The discussed findings demonstrate how personal narratives can provide in-sight into individual experiences and also tell us something about the cultural background.

In addition, it is important to know that digital discourse reduces certain aspects of a conversation, such as *acting*, which are, according to authors of CuDA, relevant for understanding. Also, the principle of *dwelling* depends on the conversation topic and cannot be generally used. As in the case of the ex-ample used in this article, the environment and location of the people played a role in the sense that surrogacy is legally impossible in Germany.

However, other principles, such as *feelings* and *being*, become more impor-tant in online settings. As Polletta & Jasper (2001) have pointed out, online con-versations ask for more intimacy and individuals trying to find their place in the digital world. Furthermore, to some extent personal interlocutions are ex-pressed a lot quicker in digital discourse, such as telecollaborative projects, in which time is often limited and less outer distractions occur, such as finding groups and physically working on a project with someone, for example looking for writing material.

Yet, this example also demonstrates limitations because only one perspec-tive is being viewed due to the amount of speech time given to the Israeli stu-dent. In addition, the topic of surrogacy also limits the interaction with others, since this is a very specific thematic field which is on the one hand not yet rele-vant to the German students and on the other hand it is not an issue in Germany because it is illegal.

Due to these limitations, future studies in this field need to analyze and discuss a broader thematical field and also a more intense conversation between the majority of interlocutors.

Nevertheless, having access to personal narratives can be a way to understand different discourses with a focus on culture and language, especially in telecollaborations of teachers in training, since this field is still relatively new and teachers' perception of the world will also be carried on to the students' world view.

References

Amott, P. (2018) Identification – a process of self-knowing realised within narrative practices for teacher educators during times of transition. *Professional Development in Education*, 44(4), 476–91. https://doi.org/10.1080/1941 5257.2017.1381638.

Amott, P. (2021). Narrative practices in developing professional identities: Issues of objectivity and agency. *London Review of Education*, 19(1), 11, 1–16. https://doi.org/10.14324/LRE.19.1.11.

Bauman, Z. (2000). *Liquid Modernity*. Polity Press.

Benwell, B. & Stokoe, E. (2011). *Discourse and Identity*. Edinburgh University Press. 10.1017/CBO9780748626533.

Bös, B., Kleinke, S., Mollin, S., & Hernández, N. (2018). *The Discursive Construction of Identities On- and Offline: Personal – Group – Collective*. John Benjamins Publishing Company.

Butler, J. (2006). *Gender trouble: Feminism and the subversion of identity*. Routledge.

Byram, M. (1997). *Teaching and assessing intercultural communicative competence*. Multilingual Matters.

Byram, M. (2009). Evaluation and/or Assessment of Intercultural Competence. In: A. Hu & M. Byram (Eds.), *Intercultural competence and foreign language learning Models, empiricism, assessment* (pp. 215–234). Gunter Narr Verlag.

Byram, M., Gribkova, B., & Starkey, H. (2002). *Developing the Intercultural Dimension in Language Teaching: A Practical Introduction for Teachers*. Council of Europe.

Carbaugh, D. (2007). Cultural Discourse Analysis: Communication Practices and Intercultural Encounters. *Journal of Intercultural Communication Research*, 36, 167–182.

Chinokul, S. (2021). Exploring the role of identity construction, teaching skills, and professional discourse & awareness: A study from a language methodology course for EFL preservice teachers. *LEARN Journal: Language Education and Acquisition Research Network*, 14(2), 427–450.

Clandinin, D.J., Pushor, D. & Orr, A.M. (2007). Navigating sites for narrative inquiry. *Journal of Teacher Education*, 58(1), 21–35. https://doi.org/10.1177/00 22487106296218.

Gee, J. P. (2015). *Social Linguistics and Literacies – Ideology in Discourses*, 5th Ed. Routledge.

Kilian, D. (2016). Providing 21st Century Skills through Telecollaboration 2.0: Uniting Technology Enhanced Language Learning with Intercultural Communication at the University Level. *MA TESOL & Applied Linguistics (Distance Learning)*.

Li, L. (2020). Novice Teachers' Discursive Construction of Their Identity: Insights from Foreign Language Classrooms. *Iranian Journal of Language Teaching Research*, 8(3), 57–76, 10.30466/IJLTR.2020.120934

Norton, B. (2000). *Identity and Language Learning – Gender, Ethnicity and Educational Change*. Pearson Education Limited.

Polletta, F. & Jasper, J. M. (2001). Collective identity and social movements. *Annual Review of Sociology*, 27, 283–305. doi: 10.1146/annurev.soc.27.1.283.

Richards, K. (2006). »Being the Teacher«: identity and classroom conversation. *Applied Linguistics*, 27(1). pp. 51–77. doi:10.1093/applin/ami041

Salinas, D. & Ayala, M. (2018). EFL Student-Teachers' Identity Construction: A Case Study in Chile. *HOW Journal*, 25(1), 33–49. https://doi.org/10.19183/ho w.25.1.380

Salonen, E. (2018). Constructing personal identities online: Self-disclosure in popular blogs. In: B. Bös, S. Kleinke, S. Mollin, N. Hernández (2018). *The Discursive Construction of Identities On- and Offline – Personal Group Collective*, 78, 57–79. DOI: 10.1075/dapsac.78.

Savva, M. (2017). Learning to teach culturally and linguistically diverse students through cross-cultural experiences. *Intercultural Education*, 28(3), 269–282.

Selting, M. et al. (1998). Gesprächsanalytisches Transkriptionssystem (GAT). *Linguistische Berichte 173*, 91–122.

Vygotsky, L. S. & Cole, M. (1978). *Mind in society: The development of higher psychological processes*. Harvard University Press.

Waldman, T., Harel, E., & Schwab, G. (2016). Getting their feet wet: trainee EFL teachers in Germany and Israel collaborate online to promote their telecollaboration competence through experiential learning. In: S. Jager, M. Kurek, & B. O'Rourke (Eds.), *New directions in telecollaborative research and practice: selected papers from the second conference on telecollaboration in higher education* (pp. 179–184). Research-publishing.net.

Waldman, T., Harel, E. & Schwab, G. (2019). Extended Telecollaboration Practice in Teacher Education: Towards Pluricultural and Plurilingual Proficiency. *European Journal of Language Policy*, 11(2), 167–185.

Zembylas, M. (2003). Emotions and Teacher Identity: A poststructural perspective. *Teachers and Teaching*, 8(1), 213–238. https://doi.org/10.1080/13540600 309378

Teaching Practices

Sense-making in the Production Process of Online Learning Materials

Michael Krüger

1. The initial situation: the IDEN project and the INEMA study program

IDEN stands for *International Digital Education Network* and is a three-year project funded by the German Academic Exchange Service (DAAD) since 2020. The goal of the project is to (1) develop instructional materials for asynchronous online learning situations used in the International Educational Management (INEMA) degree program and (2) develop and evaluate a production process that allows a team to create these materials collaboratively. We assumed that the creation of online learning materials is too time-consuming to be done by lecturers in addition to their daily tasks, and that effective collaboration with instructional designers could reduce their workload. The IDEN core team consists of three instructional designers specializing in text production (TP), filming (F), and learning platform design (LPD), as well as the project manager, who also takes on a partial role as an instructor.

INEMA is a Master's program offered jointly by Helwan University in Cairo and the University of Education in Ludwigsburg since 2011 (Krüger & Tulow-itzki, 2018). The 4–6 semester extra-occupational program is aimed at employees and managers in education and development cooperation. Its purpose is to develop managerial skills and competencies for cross-cultural challenges in education. The program is (a) non-consecutive (Hochschulrektorenkonferenz, 2014), i.e. students can be admitted even if they do not have a first degree in a pedagogical or business subject, and (b) application-oriented with a focus on theory-practice transfer and the promotion of students' action competence. Additionally, the target group of INEMA differs from typical students due to their life situation. They are employed (and remain so during their enrollment) and have usually already started their own families – circumstances that place high demands on the time flexibility of studies. The program is designed to prepare graduates to take on leadership roles in education – for example, as a school principal, in the management of a non-governmental organization, or in a senior position in a ministry.

Approximately 21 students, from 10 to 15 different countries per cohort, come together six times for 10-day learning periods, alternating between the universities in Ludwigsburg and Cairo[1]. During these »attendance phases«, great emphasis is placed on intercultural learning. Lessons are very interactive, and German-Egyptian teaching tandems carry out the teaching. Students are asked to think about management problems in their workplace and try to apply the models they have learned in their course work. By sharing concepts and revealing underlying assumptions, they learn »through differences« – which is the program's motto[2]. The phases of face-to-face learning are prepared and followed up by online learning phases, where course content and assignments are offered. The IDEN project aims to optimize these online phases. However, to understand their full function within the constructive alignment of the IN-EMA program (Biggs & Tang, 2011), it is necessary to emphasize that the online phases additionally serve to prepare students for their academic term papers and, thus, also establish contact with a base of academic literature.

It should not be ignored that the travelling required to participate in the attendance phases leaves a significant environmental footprint[3]. The degree

---

1   The program emerged from a cooperation between Germany and the Mena region (Middle East and North Africa). Through the support of the DAAD funding line EPOS (Development Related Postgraduate Studies) it was possible to open the program to students from less privileged countries who receive a scholarship through the DAAD. Since then, students from an average of 15 different countries have participated in IN-EMA courses.

2   The principle of »learning through differences« (Krummenauer-Grasser & Schweizer, 2008) underscores the innovative power that unfolds in learning projects when people with different perspectives work together on a topic. The INEMA study program deliberately works with groups that have very different cultural and professional backgrounds. For example, an employee from the Egyptian Ministry of Education is working together with an educator from Italy, an instructional designer from Colombia and a Pakistani social worker to develop an information campaign against the burning of plastic waste in rural areas of Pakistan.

3   To travel to Ludwigsburg and back, the students collectively covered 210,000 kilometers in the summer of 2022, corresponding to CO_2 emissions of 42.7 tons. (Distance calculator: www.luftlinie.org, for CO_2 calculation: www.atmosfair.de). When travelling

program therefore plans to conduct two of the six attendance phases online (in synchronous settings) in the future.

2. Complementary learning opportunities in a blended learning format

The characteristics of the INEMA program illustrate that the opportunities and limitations of its online and attendance phases are almost complementary. For example, the online learning phases provide little opportunity to initiate exploratory learning settings or support sense-making processes (Weick 1995) among students[4]. However, due to the high cultural diversity of the participants, the face-to-face phases of the program offer outstanding opportunities for confronting one's thinking patterns with the sense-making processes of other participants. During the online phases, learning processes can be extended and accompanied over several weeks and months. Pauses between learning units can be scheduled, and the setting offers good opportunities for a systematic repetition of content. Meanwhile, attendance phases usually do not allow time for a slow and steady learning process. Other characteristics of the two phases are listed in Table 1.

Table 1

Online learning phases	Attendance phases
Possibility of planning short and sequential learning units that can be mastered alongside the demands of everyday life.	Participation in attendance phases requires time-consuming planning by students (arrangements with family and employer, travel arrangements).
Possibility of long-term learning support over several weeks or months.	Chance to provide profound learning stimuli.

---

to Egypt, distances are a bit different. Overall and on average, one can assume a CO_2 footprint of 40 tons per attendance phase.

4   Sensemaking, as defined by Weick, Sutcliffe and Obstfeld, is »the ongoing retrospective development of plausible images that rationalize what people are doing« (Weick, Sutcliff & Obstfeld, 2005, 409).

Online learning phases	Attendance phases
Good opportunities for repetition and reinforcement.	Little opportunity for repetition and reinforcement.
Opportunity to become familiar with basic terms and models of the subject area.	Limited opportunities for systematic introduction and grounding of basic concepts.
Hardly any opportunities for the shared process of sense-making. Solitary learning carries the risk of becoming stuck in one's thought patterns.	Excellent opportunities for shared sense-making by applying theoretical knowledge to real practical cases and comparing different participants' solutions.
Difficulties in activating learning. Higher demands on the self-motivation and discipline of learners.	High student motivation to learn. This is likely due to group work and active involvement.
Reduced environmental, organizational, time and financial burden.	Higher environmental, organizational, time and financial burden.

3. Consequences for the fit of online materials into the given setting of learning

The complementary characteristics of the two learning phases prompted us to not try to imitate attendance phases in an online setting. We felt it made more sense to build on the specific strengths of online teaching, and thereby compensate for some of the weaknesses of face-to-face teaching. First, however, we documented some of the requirements for online learning that arise from the specific structure of an in-service degree program:

Start from scratch and increase the pace: Since learners come from different professional fields (kindergarten, school, vocational training, university, educational administration, human resources management in companies, etc.) and no common expertise can be assumed, learning units must always start at a »basic level«. However, learners are already trained in scientific/academic thinking and the organizing of their learning process, and therefore, fast and self-directed learning can be expected.

Time-boxing: Since learners study parallel to their family and work commitments, learning units must be easy to schedule. Regular and short learning phases are easier for students to organize than weakly structured learning scenarios.

Singular learning: During online learning phases, learners join from up to 12 different time zones. Synchronous learning scenarios must therefore be used very sparingly. Asynchronous networking also quickly reaches its limits, increasing learners' dependence on each other's learning pace. Conflicts arising from broken agreements cannot be adequately resolved in the online setting. However, consultations with teachers are possible.

Reference to face-to-face teaching: The online teaching materials do not stand alone. They serve as a preparation for the face-to-face lessons and/or tie in with them. The content covered in the attendance phases must be considered when designing the online learning units.

Constructive alignment: The online teaching materials also prepare students for their academic papers. Thus, another function of the online materials is to introduce students to the literature in the respective field of knowledge.

4. The function of online teaching materials in the light of Bloom's Taxonomy

To determine the function of our online learning units, we used Bloom's Taxonomy as a guide in its revised version of Krathwohl (Krathwohl, 2002). This heuristic divides learning processes into *remembering*, *understanding*, *applying*, *analyzing*, *evaluating*, and *creating*. This taxonomy has become well-known in higher education teaching methodology because a list of verbs is assigned to each learning stage, which can be used to formulate learning goals at the corresponding stage. (For critique, see Furst, 1981; Pring, 1971)

In the IDEN project, we have essentially been inspired by the postulate of Bloom's Taxonomy that levels should not be skipped. Learning at higher taxonomy levels cannot occur if there is no opportunity to go through the lower levels. This undoubtedly highlights the dilemma of a non-consecutive Master's program: on the one hand, learning must always start at the first taxonomy level since no common prior knowledge on the part of the learning group can be assumed, and on the other hand, the Master's level requires learning successes at the high and highest learning levels. This particular design makes non-consecutive Master's programs structurally vulnerable in two ways. First, the dilemma can lead to a trivialization of the degree program if higher levels of learning are not sufficiently pursued. The second danger is when lower learning levels are skipped, learning at higher levels is demanded without sufficient preparation. The resulting learning design can lead to a recognizable loss of motivation. It might also happen that learning deficits at lower levels go unnoticed, and knowledge at higher levels is merely imitated. Especially in areas of knowledge close to everyday life, such as organizing or managing, discussions may be held with little analytical insight and, in the worst case, are limited entirely to the co-creation of truisms. Providing learning materials that systematically promote learning at the lower taxonomy levels and focusing on terms and theoretical concepts during the online phases could be one way to avoid the two dangers mentioned above. New theoretical terms and models can be used to gain new perspectives on practice if they have been understood in a sufficiently differentiated manner. This goal can be pursued online. The higher taxonomy levels must be stimulated, too, because otherwise new knowledge cannot be integrated into existing knowledge (Arnold & Schüssler, 2010). This goal can be pursued in the attendance phases.

5. The inner structure of an online unit

Given the learning circumstances of INEMA students, the online units are time-boxed. To facilitate student planning, the learning process is divided into sections, and the duration is known by the students in advance. For such a section, we set a learning time of 45 to 90 minutes and called it a *unit*. Of course, the scheduled times are approximates and will vary with the individual student. For the further fine structuring of the units, we used the principles of adult education (Knowles, 1980) and their implementation of what has been called the *Sandwich Teaching Strategy* (Feldmann, 2007) as a guideline. The actual learning stimulus is thus prepared by an introduction or pre-activation that allows learners to build on their prior knowledge. It is followed by a task that requires active engagement with the subject matter. Supplemented by information that serves as orientation in the learning process (naming the learning objectives, references to further literature, etc.), this results in a prototypical structure of an online unit (see Table 2). The different parts of a unit were called *chapters*, and each has a time duration that must be considered when calculating the total length of the unit. The time duration of a chapter can range from one minute (e.g., for reading the learning objectives) to 40 minutes (e.g., for elaborating on the learning subject).

Table 2

Chapter of standard unit	Description	Reason	Approximate time for processing
1. Learning objectives for this unit	Approx. 1 to 5 objectives usually on the first two levels of Bloom's taxonomy	Transparency of the pedagogical structure to facilitate self-directed learning	1 min.
2. Introductory text (max. 150 characters)	A text that exemplifies the relevance of the topic	Facilitating learning by contextualizing, emotionalizing, or connecting to prior knowledge	1 min.
3. Overview of unit chapters	Table with links that lead to the chapters	Transparency of the pedagogical structure to facilitate self-directed learning	1 min.
4. Pre-activation or intermediate reflection (if a topic is extended over several units).	For example, Advanced Organizer, a test of prior knowledge, and a prompt for participants to describe their own experience with the topic	Establishing a link to prior knowledge. Opportunity to stimulate asynchronous discussions	10 to 20 min.
5. Learning object (e.g.: teaching input)	Presentation of new knowledge	Acquisition of new knowledge	15 to 40 min.
6. Learner activation	Active acquisition of knowledge through repetition, paraphrasing, or application	Acquisition of new knowledge, opportunity to stimulate asynchronous discussions	10 to 20 min

Chapter of standard unit	Description	Reason	Approximate time for processing
7. Summary and Outlook	Interim conclusion, reference to learning objectives, outlook on the following unit	Stimulating reflection on learning outcomes	1 min
8. Further resources	List of all sources mentioned in the unit and links to further resources	Possibility for consolidation of knowledge after the unit	1 min
9. Feedback	Possibility for immediate comment	Opportunity to stimulate asynchronous discussions and to improve the unit	5 min
Total			45 to 90 min

The detailed standard scheme aims to facilitate self-directed learning as efficiently as possible. It serves as a checklist, but not every chapter in every unit was implemented exactly according to this scheme. In some cases, the introductory text and the pre-activation (Chapters 2 and 4) were combined within an introductory video. It also happened that the teaching input was so complex that intermediate activations were inserted. As a result, chapters 5 and 6 were merged. In the case of deviations, the standard scheme helped to check whether the alternative solutions were equivalent to the original outline, and thus achieved the intended outcome just as well.

A second purpose of working with a standard scheme was to consider all time resources without overlooking any learning activities. Initially, we tended to consider only the three main chapters – pre-activation, learning object, and activation – when calculating time. This undermined our intention of timeboxing.

6. The design of the online learning materials

Oral presentations can play an important role in face-to-face classes, but online learning materials, in our experience, must rely primarily on written, audiovisual, or graphic presentations. This applies to all chapters of the standard unit, particularly to the presentation of the learning objective (i.e. the teaching input). Therefore, it was important to consider a graphic design that supports the learning process, or at least avoids any hurdles. It was essential that our learning material should facilitate a quick visual orientation, including a simple user guidance intended to prevent any feelings arising of being »lost in navigation«.

To ensure a clear structure, IDEN uses several design elements and specifications that are consistently applied to all units:

- Texts that appear directly in the unit – explanations of tasks, user notes, reader's guides or summaries – are kept short and do not exceed 100 words. Extended notes, e.g., notes used as learning objects or further resources, are visible as links or thumbnails to avoid »deserts of words«.
- Even short texts usually come with an icon, a graphic symbol indicating the character of the following text (an overview, a task, a summary, etc. See examples in illustration 1).
- All links open in a separate window to allow learners to return to the unit by simply closing the window. The only exceptions are links that navigate within the unit (chapter overview) or that lead to another unit if the preceding one has been completed.
- All graphic learning elements, such as animated videos, presentations, learning maps, etc., follow a style guide (see IDEN-Webpage, link in footnote 1) that defines the primary and secondary colors to be used. The color scheme is based on the corporate designs of the two involved universities.
- The layout of the units is vertical, i.e. progressing forward is achieved by scrolling down.

Illustration 1: Examples of icons illustrating the characteristics of text block following. (For all icons see download link in footnote[5]).

Learning goal	Reflection	Repetition
Definition	Discussion	Summary
Instruction	Transfer to practice	Further Resources

In addition to these general specifications, each unit follows an identical framework design:

Table 3

Design element	Description
Learning map	All units of a module are displayed as symbols on a learning map. Clicking on one of the symbols leads to the corresponding unit, whose chapters appear below the map. (The learning map is explained in more detail below.)
Unit title	Each unit has a meaningful title, indicating its learning content. The title is formatted as »Heading 1«.
Chapter	Each chapter has a meaningful title formatted as »Heading 2«. Besides the chapter headings, there are no other headings on this level.
Learning objectives and unit symbol	Each unit starts with a unit symbol, also found on the learning map (see below). The unit's goals are displayed by hovering the mouse over the symbol.
Introductory text	The short text is consistently given the heading »About this Unit« and preceded by the icon »Overview«.

---

5   https://www.ph-ludwigsburg.de/fakultaet-1/institut-fuer-bildungsmanagement/international-educational-leadership-and-management/iden-international-digital-education-network

Design element	Description
Tabular overview of the unit chapter	The tabular overview is located to the right of the introductory text against a slightly colored background.
Summary and Outlook	The text always bears the heading »Summary« and is introduced by the corresponding icon.
Further resources	This chapter is always titled »Further Resources« and is introduced by a »book« icon.
Feedback	This chapter is consistently headed »Your Comments«.

The design of the three main chapters (pre-activation, learning impulse, activation) is also based on the design specifications. However, the specifications are less schematic.

- All main chapters begin with a meaningful heading
- Icons can be used to illustrate texts (a total of 25 icons are available, see download link in footnote 1). However, if the chapter already contains a graphic element (e.g., a mind map that illustrates the structure of the subject matter in advance, or an embedded video whose preview image is visible in the unit), the icon can be omitted.

7. Learning maps

A learning map is the module's capstone and it summarizes the pedagogical and design considerations. The map is a picture (a photo or an illustration) representing the course's topic. A module on »Education Marketing« can be visualized by a marketplace, while the introductory course »Toolbox for Your Studies« depicts an airplane that needs to be loaded for the start of one's study trip (see graphic 2). In this background image, 20 symbols are placed, each symbol representing one of the 20 units of the course. The arrangement of the icons indicates the learning path, and the map is an advanced organizer that provides an overview of the course content. The map allows free navigation between units and encourages students to discover what is behind the symbols.

Illustration 2: The Learning Map. The objects on the bridge represent individual units, e.g. the alarm clock corresponds to the Time Management unit.

The symbols can be clicked on to access the corresponding unit, which appears below the map. Even while working on a unit, users continue to have access to the map by scrolling up to the top of the page. This visual navigation provides a clear structure even when additional optional units are added to the course. Furthermore, optional learning paths, including possible branches and side paths, can be easily visualized on the map. The learning map and the uniform design of the learning units thus jointly enable easy orientation and encourage explorative and self-directed learning.

8. The production steps of the online teaching materials

The descriptions mentioned above regarding the teaching materials' external form, length, learning level and the reference to the attendance phases, were indispensable for the shared understanding of the desired output. On this basis, we were able to define steps of a joint production process and set criteria for the intermediate results to be achieved. Of course, we were able to draw on concepts for the production process of online learning materials (Conole

& Oliver, 2007; Hoidn & Klemenčič, 2020). However, we found that we had to concretize and specify them considerably for our individual purposes.

1. The first step of our production process is a one-page outline of topics to be covered in the course. In addition, learning objectives for the course are formulated according to Bloom's Taxonomy. The objectives refer to a certain level of learning that students should have achieved before writing their academic paper (and which should enable them to do this). We formulated approximately three to five objectives per course. Instructors and course supervisors were responsible for this goal setting. At IDEN, we implemented this step through online meetings with lecturers from our partner universities, where together we created mind maps. Later, the learning objectives of the courses were discussed and further defined in weekly meetings.

2. The outline was followed by a rough planning of the attendance phase including the preparatory activities to be integrated into the upstream online phase (e.g., group assignments, presentations by the students, etc.). This planning was done by the lecturers of the course.

3. In a third step, the approximate list of essential literature to be presented in the online units was determined. Since the texts were to be made directly available to the students, copyright regulations had to be observed. In Germany, a maximum of 15% of a title may be copied and made available to a limited group for teaching purposes. Sometimes, additional book titles had to be considered to create a literature base that could be made fully available online. Student assistants could do the literature research, but the final decision was with the responsible lecturers.

4. The detailed planning of the online units was done with an Excel template that we created to support this step (see download link in footnote 1). This step aims (a) to define a learning path, i.e., an order in which the planned topics can be taught, (b) to name the individual units, (c) to define the learning objectives of the units, and (d) to assign the texts to the respective units. This planning was the responsibility of the lecturers of the course as well.

5. It has worked well for us to begin the construction of each unit with a summary of its textual basis. A well-written summary reflects the overall structure and content of the original text and sets a focus by paraphrasing and omitting passages. It is successful if it (a) does not distort the original text and (b) contains the information that will help achieve the unit's goals. The instructional designer for text production (TP) undertook this step. How-

ever, since their summary could lead to a shift in the unit's objectives, this was done in close consultation with the lecturers of the course.

6. Based on the text summary and the set learning objectives, the next step included a decision on the form of the learning object of the unit (Chapter 5 of the standard unit). Choices included presentations, film recordings, podcasts, HP5 graphics, screencasts, animated films and other options. The goal of this step was to provide an audiovisual presentation of the synopsis while offering some variety to the students. Depending on the choice, the text summary needed to be revised, shortened and adapted to fit the requirements of the chosen presentation medium. This was also a task for the specialist in text production.

7. The final creation of the learning object was done by members of the production team. Depending on its form, this was either completed by the specialist responsible for the learning platform (e.g., when creating a H5P graphic) or by the film specialist. Student assistants also contributed and, again, the creation process was supervised by the lecturers. It proved helpful to work with a web-based editing tool (e.g., Filestage), through which drafts could be shared with the entire group and in which editing requests could be easily documented.

8. In parallel with step 7, a decision about the form of activation (chapter 6 of the standard unit) had to be made. Choices included passing a multiple-choice test, creating a personal learning graphic, formulating a forum post, recording learning outcomes in a private learning journal, and other possibilities. This step was usually performed by the LPD.

9. Once the learning objective and the subsequent activation were defined, the preparatory activity (chapter 4 of the standard unit) could be developed. Personal learning objectives or prior experience with the topic could be enquired into. Review exercises were also an option to consolidate prior knowledge and prepare students for what followed. The technical implementation was done by the LPD.

10. In the final step, the learning objectives, introduction, overview, summary, resources, and feedback (Chapters 1 to 3 and 7 to 9) were created by the LPD and the introduction and outro (Chapters 2 and 7) were formulated by the instructional designer for text production (TP).

Through this sequence of steps, we produced teaching materials systematically and were able to locate difficulties in the production process. However, we are far from the end of our learning process and are continually changing and im-proving our methods.

9. Conclusion

Experience to date shows that the production of online teaching materials is a time-consuming process, not only in the operative creation of the materials, but also in the collaborative sense-making process within the team of lectur-ers and instructional designers. It involves a constant risk of production steps having to be repeated to correct mistakes or approach topics from alternative angles. A misunderstanding between two people in the production chain can result in a doubled workload for some or all of the chain. For example, we en-countered that, initially, the graphic designer interpreted educational scenes via imagery that was very reminiscent of primary and secondary schooling, rather than of higher education. The human figures portrayed were of different sizes and reinforced a clearly recognizable power difference between teachers and students. This did not align with our target group, and the misunderstand-ing only became clear after the first visualizations were already completed. It took extensive communication about the characteristics of the course and the target group to unify and synchronize our mental models. We had to develop a common language, and define exactly what we meant by each term, e.g. what a course, a unit, a chapter, or a map was, in order to be able to communicate our ideas with each other. It was also crucial to design the units from the foun-dation of a common text in order to be able to proceed with a division of labor at all. Here, it was of great benefit to have the new role of an instructional de-signer for text production, a role we had not yet thought of at the beginning of the project.

The specifications presented in this article regarding the language, func-tion, design, and creation process of online materials has helped us to realize collaborative production. Nevertheless, the model presented here is certainly not the only way to develop teaching materials and there may be other ways to design instructional materials to support learning. The original intention of the project, i.e. to relieve lecturers of the production of teaching materials by establishing a production process based on the division of labor, was achieved. However, we had to realize that we had underestimated the extent of the neces-sary sense-making procedures in the team, that is, the shared understanding of *what* we were doing, *why* we were doing it, and for *which* problem we were developing a solution. As a result, a production process was created that relieved the lecturers and further enriched the students.

Online courses are, in all their parts, steps in a mediation and translation process that begin with the text basis and reach a preliminary end with the student's creation of their scientific paper. Each intermediate step – the objectives, the summary, the learning object, the activation, etc. – can be understood as an »immutable mobile« (Latour, 2003), that is, as an artifact with its own meaning, that transforms the connotation of the previous step and prepares for the link in the chain that follows. Thus, the production of online learning materials emerges as a chain of sense-making and sense-transforming processes.

What has been postulated several times for e-learning, in general, seems to be confirmed for the creation of online teaching materials: e-learning follows the same rules as regular face-to-face teaching and has no specific e-learning pedagogy (Arnold, 2006). However, pedagogical principles need much more attention, as carelessness can more easily lead to student dropouts and a loss of retention. Exploring the challenges of designing technology-enhanced, asynchronous learning processes therefore offers an excellent opportunity to understand more precisely what we do in teaching.

References

Arnold, R. (Ed.) (2006). *eLearning-Didaktik*. Schneider-Verlag.

Arnold, R. & Schüßler, I. (Eds.) (2010). *Ermöglichungsdidaktik. Erwachsenenpädagogische Grundlagen und Erfahrungen*. 2nd Ed. Schneider.

Biggs, J.B. & Tang, C.S. (2011). *Teaching for quality learning at university. What the student does*. 4th Ed. Maidenhead: McGraw-Hill Society for Research into Higher Education & Open University Press (SRHE and Open University Press imprint).

Conole, O. (Ed.) (2007). *Contemporary perspectives in e-learning research. Themes, methods and impact on practice*. Routledge (Open and flexible learning series).

Feldmann, K.A. (2007). Identifying exemplary teachers and teaching: Evidence from student ratings. In: R.P. Perry & J.C. Smart (Eds.), *The scholarship of teaching and learning in higher education. An evidence-based perspective* (pp. 93–129). Springer.

Furst, E. J. (1981). Bloom's Taxonomy of Educational Objectives for the Cognitive Domain: Philosophical and Educational Issues. *Review of Educational Research*, 51(4), 441–453. https://doi.org/10.3102/00346543051004441

Hochschulrektorenkonferenz (2004). *Bologna-Reader. Texte und Hilfestellungen zur Umsetzung der Ziele des Bologna-Prozesses an deutschen Hochschulen.* Online: https://www.hrk.de/fileadmin/redaktion/hrk/02-Dokumente/02-10-Publikationsdatenbank/Beitr-2004-08_Bologna-Reader_I.pdf, accessed 04.08.2022.

Hoidn, S. & Klemenčič, M. (Eds.) (2020). *The Routledge international handbook of student-centered learning and teaching in higher education.* Routledge (Routledge international handbooks).

Knowles, M. (1980). *The modern practice of adult education: From pedagogy to andragogy.* Association Press.

Krathwohl, D. R. (2002). A Revision of Bloom's Taxonomy: An Overview. *Theory Into Practice*, 41(4), 212–218. https://doi.org/10.1207/s15430421tip4104_2.

Krüger M. & Tulowitzki P. (2018). Grenzüberschreitender Bildungstransfer durch Bildungsprojekte – Transferindizien aus einem internationalen Weiterbildungsstudiengang. *ZHWB Zeitschrift Hochschule und Weiterbildung*, 2018, 2.

Krummenauer-Grasser, A. & Schweizer, G. (2008). Das Prinzip »Lernen am Unterschied«. In: U. Müller, G. Schweizer, & S. Wippermann (Eds.), *Visionen entwickeln – Bildungsprozesse wirksam steuern – Führung professionell gestalten* (pp. 93–103). Bertelsmann.

Latour, B. (2003). *Science in action. How to follow scientists and engineers through society.* 11th print. Harvard University Press.

Ormell, C. P. (1974). Bloom's Taxonomy and the Objectives of Education. *Educational Research*, 17(1), 3–18. https://doi.org/10.1080/0013188740170101.

Pring, R. (1971). Bloom's Taxonomy: A philosophical critique (2). *Cambridge Journal of Education*, 1(2), 83–91. https://doi.org/10.1080/0305764710010205.

Weick, K.E. (1995). *Sensemaking in organizations.* Sage Publications.

Weick, K., Sutcliffe, K. M., & Obstfeld, D. (2005). Organizing and the process of sensemaking. *Organization Science*, 16(4), 409–421.

Students' Perspectives on Digital and International Virtual Academic Cooperation
Introduction

Anselm Böhmer

The project Digital and International Virtual Academic Cooperation (DIVA) took place in 2020 and 2021. It brought together academics and students from Israel, Australia, and Germany to learn together and develop individual and joint skills in culturalized difference and digital collaboration. The DIVA project, in particular, aimed to expand existing learning opportunities and create new collaborations in the area of digital teaching formats at the participating universities in connection with international networks of scholars and students. We explicitly drew on the extensive experience of individual scholars and their many years of collaboration in different international research and teaching contexts. The project was directly linked to the universities' internationalization and digitization policies and aimed to promote the development of intercultural and teamwork skills between students and scholars.

Thus, with DIVA we developed and tested two comprehensive course components (synchronous/asynchronous and virtual/physical) and embedded them in the respective curricula and administration procedures. Co-teaching and peer learning as well as courses offered jointly with the international cooperation partners were the central building blocks of this project. The courses were developed in direct cooperation with international partners and were generated according to the needs of the students and their learning and social circumstances. All parts of the project were based on four guiding principles: digitization of teaching, methodological anchoring in the curriculum, fostering virtual and blended mobility, and promotion of intercultural competence.

This approach implies that students are deeply involved in the development, implementation, and evaluation of the project and its teaching components. It is therefore logical that the students should also be involved in the reflection on this project here in this volume. Two of them – Ms. Tipura Sundari and Mr. Wang, both Master students at Charles Darwin University – were kind enough to share their experiences and pedagogical reflections with us. You will find their reflections below.

Two of their ideas will be highlighted in this introduction: the importance of digital learning (Tripura Sundari) and intercultural collaboration (Wang). Both aspects are definitely crucial for the success of the international virtual academic exchange, as the program line of the project funding is titled[1]. As both students show in their texts, digital learning and intercultural cooperation are closely related in higher education, if not in every aspect of education. There is now a kind of »new normal« in applying digital platforms, tools, and processes in international learning (see also Bolaji's chapter in this volume).

In this way, virtuality and collaboration reinforce each other by developing a culture of collaboration even when students do not know each other at the beginning of the course and may only meet online. The digital environment seems to offer so many opportunities for co-operation that, if they are used properly, they can support experiences of intense and fruitful collaboration.

Nonetheless, there are some cultural and technical challenges in this kind of learning collaboration. As can be seen from the students' texts, there is always a need for some form of support from the scholars. This is also the case in higher education, as can be taken from the account in the following section. The students' experiences and suggestions are therefore of immense importance for the understanding of the DIVA project, as well as for digital learning in intercultural cooperation in general. This is also the reason why we are so grateful for their contributions.

---

1   IVAC – International Virtual Academic Exchange by the German Academic Exchange Service (DAAD).

A World of Tomorrow
The Perspectives of Online Learners on Digital Teaching and Learning

Lalitha Tripura Sundari

1. Introduction

When I decided to do a master's degree in global education after almost a decade after graduating from university, I did not realize what a journey I was embarking on. I thought this was going to be a walk in the park. Why shouldn't I do this? That is what I had thought. As I was an ICT professional and a corporate trainer by profession, I thought I was carved out for the digital world and took it for granted that the learning world was calling for my expertise.

However, I was in for a surprise! Online learning was new and different. It was nowhere near as easy as I thought, and though I had the technological knowledge and media tools to support me, it turned out that there was a more challenging and lonely life of learning ahead of me than I had anticipated.

A learning phase revealed itself that was unavoidable and intimidating. Many a time, I felt this as a self-inflicted pain that, far from bearing any immediate – fruit, did not even make any sense to me, with a piled-up list of missed deadlines on assignments and academic records that left me feeling awful and agonized.

Then why continue learning? And why the digital life? (I asked myself). The only answer I could give myself was that it was possible! It was very much possible. There was a wealth of knowledge out there, and with its abundance it was calling me to take a dip in it.

Getting into it wasn't difficult, but keeping myself afloat was the real challenge. I was able to contact my professors during my hit-on-wall situations, seeking guidance or support, or just rambling away -sometimes my conversation went along the lines of repent and remorse, and I started to think I had made a terrible mistake enrolling myself in this course.

Meanwhile, as usual, my real world was going about its business, ruthlessly demanding and needy. And like a hamster in a wheel, I forgot all about my need to learn and went about my chores, and learning, education, and study all took a back seat.

While I was caught up in meeting deadlines, I received unread emails from my teachers. They followed up and asked about my progress, gently pushing me to keep going. Their encouragement inspired me to be brave, pick up my pen, and continue learning, sharing and growing.

This was a digital learning breakthrough for me. I didn't have to go through a difficult academic process. Academia quietly came to me, motivating me to move forward. The universities reached out, urging students like me to keep progressing and stay ahead.

This chapter is written to share my experiences and observations as a digital learner and corporate trainer, with the help of reference to the relevant research literature to back up my analysis.

2. Digital learning background

We cannot hide from information technology. Every living person is exposed to waves of digital information, and can no longer choose freely to ignore it. Teachers cannot therefore avoid information technology; and likewise, students cannot escape digital learning. Technology and digital learning are here to stay and are the way forward. University education is widely accessible now beyond national borders, pandemic life having paved the way for this from 2020. National borders are dissolving with globalization. Today, digital technology is deeply integrated into university teaching and learning, from the institutional provision of learning management systems and journals to the widespread use of word processing, email, Google, and Wikipedia.

It is now considered a routine part of academic study and campus life for students to use digital technology at universities, an unremarkable feature of contemporary higher education. The use of digital technology outside of higher education continues to be portrayed as a force for change and reform. As a result of growing up »digital«, today's students are more dependent on digital technology than in the past (Prensky, 2012).

However, the »disruptive« nature of new technology and the need for increasingly digitally attuned students are causing universities to struggle (Losh, 2014). The overarching sense is a fundamental re-alignment and reform of university teaching and learning along digital lines. This then leaves us with the question of what to do about the other different types of atypical learning formats that are being introduced with the expansion of digital technology and the disruption in curriculum and structure that students are expected to negotiate. How much of classroom structure needs to be rediscovered?

3. Digital learning and teaching – technology in higher education and other learning institutions

Online learning is prevalent in today's educational environments and is supported by virtual learning environments (VLEs) such as Moodle™, Sakai™, or Blackboard™. The new VLEs are important elements of the new educational experience that addresses all aspects of user activity, courses, and communication management. In addition, VLEs are being used at all levels of education. Among the choices in highly interactive multimedia content, games are positioned as an excellent complement to traditional education, as they have several exciting features from a pedagogical perspective.

As a corporate trainer for cloud software programs, I primarily teach online. As part of the pieces of training conducted periodically, students are assessed on the last day of the learning program by undergoing configuration setup and answering multiple-choice questions. Interestingly, in normal life professionally and technically well-versed students, who invest their time in learning state-of-the-art cloud software, often have trouble accessing their learning materials using the eLearning system. At least 2 out of 10 students have difficulty accessing their online exam portals, whether they are baby boomers or generation Alpha. This makes one wonder if technology is to be blamed, or whether the cause lies with the individual student's inability to adapt to new learning methods.

Different teaching and learning strategies are required on different vertical levels[1] of an educational system to ensure effective and efficient learning. It is also the case that different formal and non-formal learning spaces require

---

1   As a result of the learning system, a student/learner expands their knowledge and enhances their skills on a horizontal level of learning. As we learn vertically, we transform

different technological and cognitive development levels. The main task and challenges consist in identifying the appropriate institutional or atypical levels and the algorithmically suitable methods regarding the age and mental characteristics of the learner. (Dostovalova, et al., 2018)

4. Is interculture a companion or conflict in order?

My participation in the transnational university project raised my awareness of various digital media tools, different representations of the same idea, and, most importantly, what languages and locational displacement can cause us to experience. Cultural differences will no longer be a barrier or a bargaining chip as we spread our wings and embrace the world. On the other hand, this will be a necessary experience that will shine through and enrich one's life. Furthermore, whether a person is Asian, Western, or European will be less critical, as a more credible picture of global existence and human relationships emerges.

Digital technology and global access constitute a tool that can make all this possible, but at the same time can potentially be a double-edged sword. If digital media and technology are utilized inefficiently, we may lose the partial aim of creating global citizens.

The concept of »multicultural education« can refer to any attempt on the part of education to respond to cultural plurality, or similar approaches, which can then be contrasted with other approaches such as »anti-racist-« ones. The basic idea behind »multicultural education« is that cultural diversity should be appreciated and reflected in the school curriculum (Ward, 2004).

5. Conclusion

Digital teaching has come to stay, irrespective of geographical location, culture, age, and social needs. We hope that by establishing a culture of good practice around digital technology as a professional body, we will see a positive change in the quality of services provided to students, which may improve students' overall digital literacy development (Podorova A., et, al., 2019).

---

how we think, absorb and understand the world and run through its layers of complexity.

Preparing the staff in higher education, and students, who are consumers of the knowledge, to be receptive to the technology stream is vital. Digital teaching must be interwoven with the classic form of learning and standardizing academic learning tools and technology is a must. When we are using more and more digital technology, class involvement techniques and appropriate forms of learning discipline need to be discovered by both educators and learners. It is critical to remember, from a pedagogical standpoint, that course delivery – whether face-to-face, blended/hybrid, or entirely online – is not an end in itself. The goal is to design effective learning (Guppy et al., 2022).

The learning field is going through a lot of changes, and this has brought with it an amalgamation of positive changes and challenging situations. As a consequence, the educational industry and higher education institutions must devise plans and policies that must be sensitive to these changes and include perspectives of faculty, students, instructional designers, and curriculum developers. Digital teaching is not a sudden and short-term need, but a kind of »gearing up« for a bigger and more novel social change. This observational study offers just a glimpse of what is possible and cannot be a conclusive work.

The DIVA project stands out as an example of taking students beyond the curriculum and classroom setup to collaborate and learn in similar ways, and the learning culture needs to adapt and develop innovative methods to take the learning to students and vice versa. We need many such examples to allow digital technology and students to depend on each other and thrive in doing so, thus creating a society with a high level of digital literacy.

In our DIVA workshop, three things stood out: (1) students from a variety of universities exchanged ideas and thoughts, (2) collaboration itself varied from formal to informal, depending on the student's country of origin, i.e., where he or she migrated for study, and (3) the media environment which participants encountered.

As this was a complete digital and online collaboration project, an interesting aspect of participation was that some of us were novices in technology usage, while others tended towards the level of experts.

Our conversation moved from awkward introductions to awesome insights about learning, global understanding, and what we knew about each other.

I felt that the spectrum of intercultural learning had developed well when every group ran through its learnings and project outcomes.

A distinctive feature of this project was that it provided students with the freedom to use the best technology for the project, encouraging exploration while at the same time providing academic support whenever needed.

References

Dostovalova, E., Simonova, A., Nazarenko, E., Maschanov, A., & Lomasko, P. (2018). Teaching in a Continuously and Dynamically Changing Digital Information and Learning Environment of a Modern University. *The New Educational Review*, 53(3), 126–141. https://doi.org/10.15804/tner.2018.53.3.11

Guppy, N., Verpoorten, D., Boud, D., Lin, L., Tai, J., & Bartolic, S. (2022). The post-COVID-19 future of digital learning in higher education: Views from educators, students, and other professionals in six countries. *British Journal of Educational Technology*, 53(6), 1750–1765. https://doi.org/10.1111/bjet.13212

Losh, E. (2014). *The War on Learning: Gaining Ground in the Digital University*. MIT Press. https://doi.org/10.7551/mitpress/9861.001.0001

Podorova, A., Irvine, S., Kilmister, M., Hewison, R., Janssen, A., Speziali, A., Balavijendran, L., Kek, M., & McAlinden, M. (2019). An important, but neglected aspect of learning assistance in higher education: Exploring the digital learning capacity of academic language and learning practitioners. *Journal of University Teaching & Learning Practice*, 16(4). https://doi.org/10.53761/1.16.4.3

Prensky, M. (2012). *Brain Gain. Technology and the Quest for Digital Wisdom*. Palgrave Macmillan.

Ward, S. (Ed.) (2004). *Education studies: A student's guide*. Taylor & Francis Group.

How to facilitate peer interactions in virtual intercultural learning
An example in the DIVA project

Xirui Wang

1. Background

In 2021, I got an opportunity to participate in an intercultural learning activity between Germany and Australia, organized by the Ludwigsburg University of Education in Germany through its DIVA project (Digital and International Virtual Academic Cooperation). During this part of the project[1], I cooperated with two Ludwigsburg students to do a comparative study on the education systems of China, Croatia, and Germany. The final product was an online presentation in front of all participants.

It was a pleasure working with the team members. However, when I reflect on my experiences in the project, I find that I could have had more opportunities to communicate with my team members and learn about their cultures.

Probably because we were all busy, there was not much opportunity for us to take some time to chat freely about each other's culture. The only virtual meeting that we had was organized by professors, who sent us to breakout rooms to meet team members after the project opening ceremony via Zoom. We quickly moved on to the discussions on our project after a few minutes of chatting. After this, we completed most of our communications through a messenger app, on which our messages were serious and mainly focused on our project. We decided on a shared structure composed of three aspects of education systems, and we worked independently to collect information on the

---

1   The other part of the DIVA-project comprised a collaboration between the Kibbutzim College of Education in Tel Aviv and Ludwigsburg University of Education in the field of language education.

countries that we each focused on. After we finished our parts, we combined the slides and concluded similarities and differences between each country's parts. In the final presentation session, some teams seemed to have had abundant discussions. However, although our team completed the work, there were not many casual chats where we could learn from and about each other beyond the project task. Surprisingly, the project was completed without abundant peer discussion or educator support, which raises my interest in the generality of such phenomena where students in an online cooperative learning program complete their tasks without many interactions, especially in an intercultural education program where social interactions could enhance mutual and cross-cultural understanding and contribute to the achievement of the goal of the program.

2. Intercultural Education

As early as 1951, prompted by the social problems after WWII, Redden and Ryan (1951) were already discussing the importance of intercultural education in promoting international understanding, reducing international conflicts, and improving international relations. However, cultural conflicts arise between countries and within states and societies in an even more radical form, which has prompted an imperative to promote intercultural education inside different societies (Jones, 1997).

To better understand the meaning of "intercultural", a comparison between "intercultural" and "multicultural" might be of some help. While multiculturalism focuses on the recognizing differences based on equality and variety, interculturalism emphasizes coexistence in diversity with an additional principle of positive interaction (Guilherme & Dietz, 2015). To summarise, intercultural education emphasizes positive interactions in a diverse and equal society.

Intercultural education can benefit the education system and the wider society. As Ghosh (2021) points out, education should help to reduce conflicts and promote social cohesion, especially during the coronavirus pandemic. Intercultural education could promote social cohesion, but there are further benefits. By addressing critical literacy and culturally responsive instructions, intercultural education could effectively improve academic achievements of students from minoritized backgrounds by challenging the inequality and discrimination they often suffer (Cummins, 2015).

Despite the benefits of intercultural education, it should be admitted that its implementation still has challenges (Steinbach, 2011). Merely celebrating the diversity of cultures is insufficient because students also need to learn how to recognize themselves (self-identity) and their relationships with their cultural backgrounds and other cultures (social identity) so that they can find their position in social relationships and make sense of their subjective experiences (Ghosh & Abdi, 2004). In addition, the prevalence of a folkloric approach in intercultural education might objectify cultures into cultural products like food and clothing at the cost of further understanding cultures (Gérin-Lajoie, 2011). While intercultural education could benefit students and a wider community, successful intercultural education is not only about celebrating folklore or the diversity of student cohorts but must also involve critical reflection on inequality and appropriate guidance from educators.

3. Virtual Learning

Alla (2005) uses "virtual learning" as an umbrella term to describe a learning process based on technology, with teachers and students possibly separated by time and place, yet more flexibility for the learning pace of individual students. The tools used for virtual learning include virtual meetings, online courses, and virtual learning environments (Kerimbayev, 2020).

Discussions on new forms of education based on technologies and the Internet started as early as the end of the 20th century. Virtual learning can make learning more efficient, individual, timely, and task-oriented (Mueller & Strohmeier, 2011). However, to realize the full potential of virtual learning, learner-centred course design and social interactions between learners are also vital, in addition to using technologies (Stiles, 2000). The advent of COVID-19 further highlights the imperative of up-skilling teachers' digital technology repertoires, which can, for instance, help to ensure that teaching activities in relatively poor areas can continue just as in metropolitan counterparts and thus improve the social equality of education (Maloney & Moorthy, 2021). During the COVID-19 pandemic, virtual learning was widely implemented, with increasing popularity in academic discussions (see, e.g., Marín-Díaz et al. (2021) or Torres Martín et al. (2021)).

An important focus of studies on virtual learning is virtual learning's potential to facilitate social interactions among students. The interactions between educators and students have been an essential consideration in developing virtual learning (Brent, 2000). However, the style of social interaction online could vary for people with different personalities (Amichai-Hamburger et al., 2002). Students' willingness and participation style could also differ between classroom and virtual learning environments (Caspi et al., 2006).

Besides focusing on social interactions, relevant research addresses the need for learning strategies, learning support, and possible obstacles. As early as 2000, Stiles (2000) noticed that virtual learning requires effective learning strategies instead of merely focusing on technology, or the learning will still be unengaging for students. Besides learning strategies, students also need training on the potential functions of virtual learning environments, educators' monitoring of their learning progress, and stable Internet connections (Marín-Díaz et al., 2021). In addition, In addition, certain obstacles to social interactions in virtual learning environments need to be addressed, such as participants not turning on cameras or microphones during a meeting and other hindrances to fluid online communication (Finlay et al., 2022).

4. Cooperative Learning

Cooperative learning, which is about organizing students to work in small groups, has been the object of a vast amount of related research worldwide (Slavin, 1989). As one type of peer learning, cooperative learning is a learning process in which students work in groups towards a goal the teacher sets with the teacher's facilitation (Topping et al., 2017). Furthermore, cooperative learning requires training in participating in and contributing to group work (Topping, 2005). Cooperative learning has been widely used in educational contexts and discussed by scholars, for example, Boud et al. (1999), Topping et al. (2011), and Thurston et al. (2010).

Cooperative learning has apparent advantages. As early as 1980, Slavin (1980) found that cooperative learning was beneficial for both the academic and affective development of students compared with traditional teaching techniques; it led, for example, to better academic achievements, consistent improvement in the relationships of students from different cultural backgrounds, more profound mutual understanding, improved self-esteem, and more positive attitudes towards school. While cooperative learning could be a beneficial practice for students, many challenges remain to be dealt with. At the beginning of cooperative learning, there should be training on interpersonal and cooperating skills (Jolliffe, 2007). In addition to structuring teams and learning tasks, the implementation of cooperative learning demands essential changes in the focus of assessments, from the current individual-centred approach to a new form of assessment and from the significant focus on cognitive skills to a combination of cognitive and non-cognitive skills such as social skills (Huber & Huber, 2008). Besides the need for more support from teachers on both group work and individual work of students, students also have more responsibilities for their learning, which could be challenging for students (Cooper, 2002).

5. Discussions

My learning path in the project was completely online, and involved a Zoom opening ceremony, office hours with professors on Zoom (optional), online group discussions (on a messenger app), and a Zoom closing meeting where each group gave a presentation. During the opening ceremony, I had the first opportunity to meet and communicate with my group members when students were sent into breakout rooms after the professors' introduction to the DIVA project. After self-introductions, our group discussion soon moved to discussions on possible topics and the separation of tasks. My group members were efficient and work-oriented. However, if there had been some casual conversation, we might have been able to get to know each other better and learn more about each other's cultures. Maybe my group members were also eager to have some personal conversational exchange, but as people meeting for the first time, they may have found it difficult to start chatting. This difficulty in initial engagement seems to align with the research of Pricope (2013), who finds that students from different backgrounds do not necessarily communicate with each other and learn about other cultures when they are on the same campus. Extra efforts might be needed to stimulate discussions among students in an intercultural education project, especially if the project is online. When students are learning online, social interactions between them need to be facilitated, and the use of cameras and microphones might need to be encouraged and checked (Finlay et al., 2022; Laffey et al., 2006). When participants from different backgrounds meet for the first time in a Zoom breakout room, it is natural that they could feel it challenging to start a casual conversation. Educators could improve peer interactions by setting some icebreaking tasks to encourage students to understand each other. During the activity time, educators might consider joining breakout rooms to check on the progress and offer support for less active members of the group. While an intercultural cooperative learning program is running, it is important to realise that students might feel much more challenged due to cultural differences. Therefore, explicitly teaching intercultural skills and group work processes before the work starts could be significant (Huber & Huber, 2008; Jolliffe, 2007).

6. Recommendations

Based on my reflections on my experiences during the DIVA project, I would like to offer some recommendations for implementing online intercultural cooperative learning projects.

Firstly, as mentioned above, educators could use icebreaking activities to involve students in initial communication and encourage peer interactions. The activities should be designed to encourage students in an online environment to interact further with each other when they are working together. Students might not necessarily interact with each other and learn about other cultures just because they are in an intercultural environment, so the actively stimulated engagement of students with each other is necessary.

Secondly, educators could monitor the progress of students. By frequently checking with students, educators could discover how they might provide spontaneous help in facilitating contact, while participants might also feel greater motivation or pressure to work hard on the project.

Thirdly, building an online learning space where students could create and design together might help to build a more cohesive community that generates a sense of belonging. A possible learning space might be a website that every student could edit. Educators could encourage students to devise web pages, publish blogs, and share resources on the website together. To effectively engage students in the website activities, educators should help students find their motivations in building a website together and offer training in the skills students will need.

To summarize, online intercultural cooperative learning certainly benefits educators, but there are also challenges. While it is possible to overcome geographical barriers through virtual learning, educators need to engage students in the learning by facilitating peer interactions, by progress checking, and by constructing shared cyberspaces like websites that every student could edit.

References

Alla, A. (2005). Analysis of the terminology used in the field of virtual learning. *Journal of Educational Technology & Society*, 8(3), 91–102.

Amichai-Hamburger, Y., Wainapel, G., & Fox, S. (2002). "On the Internet No One Knows I'm an Introvert": Extroversion, Neuroticism, and Internet Interaction. *CyberPsychology & Behavior*, 5(2), 125–128. https://doi.org/10.1089/109493102753770507

Boud, D., Cohen, R., & Sampson, J. (1999). Peer Learning and Assessment. *Assessment & Evaluation in Higher Education*, 24(4), 413–426. https://doi.org/10.1080/0260293990240405

Brent, M. (2000). Enhancing Social Interaction in Computer-Mediated Distance Education. *Journal of Educational Technology & Society*, 3(4), 1–11. http://www.jstor.org/stable/jeductechsoci.3.4.1

Caspi, A., Chajut, E., Saporta, K., & Beyth-Marom, R. (2006). The influence of personality on social participation in learning environments. *Learning and Individual Differences*, 16(2), 129–144. https://doi.org/10.1016/j.lindif.2005.07.003

Cooper, S. M. A. (2002). Classroom Choices for Enabling Peer Learning. *Theory into practice*, 41(1), 53–57. https://doi.org/10.1207/s15430421tip4101_9

Cummins, J. (2015). Intercultural education and academic achievement: a framework for school-based policies in multilingual schools. *Intercultural Education*, 26(6), 455–468. https://doi.org/10.1080/14675986.2015.1103539

Finlay, M. J., Tinnion, D. J., & Simpson, T. (2022). A virtual versus blended learning approach to higher education during the COVID-19 pandemic: The experiences of a sport and exercise science student cohort. *Journal of Hospitality, Leisure, Sport & Tourism Education*, 30, 100363. https://doi.org/10.1016/j.jhlste.2021.100363

Gérin-Lajoie, D. (2011). Multicultural education: Nothing more than folklore? *Canadian Issues*, 24–27. https://acs-metropolis.ca/wp-content/uploads/2021/04/R6BPxvD3PvAemyZ6BeEB.pdf#page=26

Ghosh, R. (2021). Can Education Contribute to Social Cohesion? In B. Lindsay (Ed.), *Comparative and International Education: Leading Perspectives from the Field* (pp. 87–104). Springer International Publishing. https://doi.org/10.1007/978-3-030-64290-7_6

Ghosh, R., & Abdi, A. A. (2004). *Education and the Politics of Difference: Canadian Perspectives*. Canadian Scholars' Press.

Guilherme, M., & Dietz, G. (2015). Difference in diversity: multiple perspectives on multicultural, intercultural, and transcultural conceptual complexities. *Journal of Multicultural Discourses*, 10(1), 1–21. https://doi.org/10.1080/17447143.2015.1015539

Huber, G. L., & Huber, A. A. (2008). Structuring Group Interaction to Promote Thinking and Learning During Small Group Learning in High School Settings. In R. M. Gillies, A. F. Ashman, & J. Terwel (Eds.), *The Teacher's Role in Implementing Cooperative Learning in the Classroom* (pp. 110–131). Springer US. https://doi.org/10.1007/978-0-387-70892-8_6

Jolliffe, W. (2007). *Cooperative learning in the classroom: Putting it into practice*. SAGE Publications Ltd, https://doi.org/10.4135/9781446213971

Jones, C. (1997). Nation, State and Diversity. In D. Coulby, J. S. Gundara, & C. Jones (Eds.), *World Yearbook of Education 1997: Intercultural Education*. Routledge. https://doi.org/10.4324/9780203080276

Kerimbayev, N. (2020). Formats of Virtual Learning. In A. Tatnall (Ed.), *Encyclopedia of Education and Information Technologies* (pp. 779–790). Springer International Publishing. https://doi.org/10.1007/978-3-030-10576-1_201

Laffey, J., Lin, G. Y., & Lin, Y. (2006). Assessing Social Ability in Online Learning Environments. *Journal of Interactive Learning Research*, 17(2), 163–177. https://www.learntechlib.org/primary/p/5981/

Maloney, K., & Moorthy, T. (2021, October 5). *How investing in tech for teachers can bring equity to education*. World Economic Forum. https://www.weforum.org/agenda/2021/10/digital-skills-teachers-education-equality/

Marín-Díaz, V., Reche, E., & Martín, J. (2021). University Virtual Learning in Covid Times. *Technology, Knowledge and Learning*, 27, 1291–1309. https://doi.org/10.1007/s10758-021-09533-2

Mueller, D., & Strohmeier, S. (2011). Design characteristics of virtual learning environments: state of research. *Computers & Education*, 57(4), 2505–2516. https://doi.org/10.1016/j.compedu.2011.06.017

Pricope, M. (2013). Challenges and benefits of intercultural education. *Euromentor Journal – Studies about education*, 4(2), 75–80. https://www.proquest.com/scholarly-journals/challenges-benefits-intercultural-education/docview/1449574620/se-2

Redden, J. D., & Ryan, F. A. (1951). *Intercultural education*. Bruce Pub. Co. http://catalog.hathitrust.org/api/volumes/oclc/1191886.html

Slavin, R. E. (1980). Cooperative Learning. *Review of educational research*, 50(2), 315–342. https://doi.org/10.3102/00346543050002315

Slavin, R. E. (1989). Research on Cooperative Learning: an international perspective. *Scandinavian Journal of Educational Research*, 33(4), 231–243. https://doi.org/10.1080/0031383890330401

Steinbach, M. (2011). Intercultural education in Quebec: Preparing teachers and students for diversity. *Canadian Issues*, 67–70. https://acs-metropolis.ca/wp-content/uploads/2019/05/CITC-2011-Spring-Printemps-L.pdf#page=69

Stiles, M. J. (2000). Effective learning and the virtual learning environment. *Proceedings: EUNIS 2000–Towards Virtual Universities*, Instytut Informatyki Politechniki Poznanskiej, Poznan, Poland.

Thurston, A., Topping, K. J., Tolmie, A., Christie, D., Karagiannidou, E., & Murray, P. (2010). Cooperative Learning in Science: Follow-up from primary to high school. *International Journal of Science Education*, 32(4), 501–522. https://doi.org/10.1080/09500690902721673

Topping, K., Buchs, C., Duran, D., & van Keer, H. (2017). *Effective Peer Learning* (1st ed.). Routledge. https://doi-org/10.4324/9781315695471

Topping, K. J. (2005). Trends in Peer Learning. *Educational Psychology*, 25(6), 631–645. https://doi.org/10.1080/01443410500345172

Topping, K. J., Thurston, A., Tolmie, A., Christie, D., Murray, P., & Karagiannidou, E. (2011). Cooperative learning in science: intervention in the secondary school. *Research in Science & Technological Education*, 29(1), 91–106. https://doi.org/10.1080/02635143.2010.539972

Torres Martín, C., Acal, C., El Homrani, M., & Mingorance Estrada, Á. C. (2021). Impact on the Virtual Learning Environment Due to COVID-19. *Sustainability*, 13(2), 582. https://www.mdpi.com/2071-1050/13/2/582

Some Perspectives

Anselm Böhmer

Having read Mrs. Tripura Sundari's and Mr. Wang's contributions, one sees that many aspects can be collated as »lessons learned«: digital learning and teaching are indeed a »new normal« of academic collaboration – at every university and even more so in international courses. There are always obstacles to be overcome, but in the end, the success of the collaboration is a question of individual skills, motivations, and well-designed opportunities and tasks. It is therefore a requirement for scholars in higher education (1) to bring with them competence in creating inclusive, supportive, and safe digital learning environments, (2) to have the knowledge and capacity to support learning processes individually and as a collaborative activity, and also (3) to be able to transfer knowledge, expertise, and digital outcomes into a set of competencies and skills that combine academic reflection and critical thinking with purposeful activities grounded in professional practice.

Both students have reflected on their experiences not only in a personal sense, but also within their academic theoretical framework. This demonstrates the importance of theoretical considerations when interacting in practical settings and project-based work-flows. Professional alliances and professionalization in general are based on theoretical reflections that help to describe, comprehend, and engage with the environment of learning, collaboration, and practice. For students, this is clearly helpful in their professionalization as (future) educators and it leads to the realization that digitization is a »quintessential aspect of any higher education sector« (Tripura Sundari) that is as supportive as it is indispensable for the training of future educators. Additionally, the collaboration of scholars and students in learning and »building an online learning space« (Wang) together marks what will be helpful for future projects. It is the academic community of scholars and students that creates professional cooperations projects, and thus develops future communities of practice.

Here, both students have shared their experiences, but have also expressed their academic approaches to becoming professionals. This shows how much DIVA has achieved, how digital learning has brought together many of the best of the participants and contributed to opening up the future for better digital collaboration – at universities and beyond.

Authors' Profiles

Stine Albers, Dr., is an assistant professor of pedagogy and didactics of elementary and primary education at Ludwigsburg University of Education, Germany. She is also head of the Department of Sachunterricht and a member of the Research Committee, making a significant contribution to both teaching and research.

Bettina Blanck, Dr., is a professor of social sciences and elementary school education at the Ludwigsburg University of Education, Germany, and a member of various committees and institutes there. With her social science expertise, she contributes to advancing educational processes and democratic participation. Her research interests include promoting deliberation in education from the beginning of learning, dealing with diversity, and developing critical reflective and questioning attitudes among teachers and learners. She has a particular focus on developing the philosophical concept of deliberatively oriented research and fostering an environment conducive to learning in which negatively valued but problem-adequate alternatives are not worthless but are also considered part of knowledge itself.

Anselm Böhmer, Dr., is a professor of general education at Ludwigsburg University of Education, Germany. His main areas of research are education in late modernity, diversity, social differences, migration, culturalization, and digital learning environments.

Stephen Bolaji, Ph.D., is a research active academic and teaches graduate programs and secondary curriculum humanities units in the Discipline of Education, Faculty of Arts and Society, Charles Darwin University, Australia. Prior to joining CDU, he was a lecturer at the Department of Educational Foundations and Counselling, Faculty of Education, University of Lagos, Nigeria.

Karen Cieri is a senior policy officer within the Northern Territory Department of Education and a graduate student at Charles Darwin University, Darwin. She has a background in psychology and systems change in education. Karen is currently completing doctorate research into collaborative and community-led ways of working.

Sarah Gaubitz, Dr., is an assistant professor of interdisciplinary subject matter education at the University of Erfurt. Department spokesperson for elementary school pedagogy and childhood research.

Illie Isso has been working as an academic staff member and program coordinator at the Professional School of Education Stuttgart-Ludwigsburg (PSE) since August 2022. In addition, he has been working as a research assistant at the Ludwigsburg University of Education (LUE) in the DAAD-funded IQ-Lab project since April 2023.
Previously, he was a research assistant at the LUE from April 2021 to September 2022 and was responsible for project management in the DAAD-funded projects DIVA and EUGEN, among others. Since May 2021, he is also a doctoral candidate in history at the Ludwigsburg University of Education. Previously, he completed his teaching degree in history, ethics, technology, and physical education with the first state exam. His research interests include history, education in the context of social inequality, diversity, inclusion, and migration.

Michael Krüger, Dr. is coordinator of the International Education Management program (INEMA) at the University of Education in Ludwigsburg. His work focuses on developing learning materials for asynchronous learning environments (project IDEN) as well as teaching organizational learning, quality management, project management and coaching.

Jon Mason, Ph.D., is an Associate Professor in Education with the Faculty of Arts & Society at Charles Darwin University (CDU), Australia, where he lectures and conducts research in the broad area of digital technology in education. Among his academic roles he is also a member of the NT Academic Centre for Cyber Security and Innovation. With a longstanding interest in international collaboration, he also holds adjunct positions at Korea National Open

University and East China Normal University. He serves on several journal editorial boards and has performed editorial roles for international projects and books. His research spans most things where digital technology and learning intersect while also pursuing a keen interest in question formulation, sensemaking, and the role of wisdom in education.

Svenja Meier is a Ph.D. student, who is doing her research on the Digital and International Virtual Academic Cooperation (DIVA) project. She is a member of the Institute for English at Ludwigsburg University of Education.

Viktoria Rieber is an academic staff member at the Institute for Sachunterricht (Science and Social Studies in primary school education) at the Heidelberg University of Education. In addition, she is doing her doctorate in the context of social science teaching at the Ludwigsburg University of Education. Her doctoral research focuses on the promotion of competencies of decision-making in the context of education for sustainable development and civic education. Her research also focuses on conceptualization as a fundamental task of education, philosophy for children and Care Work as an educational topic.

Götz Schwab, Dr., is Professor of Applied Linguistics at the Institute of English, Ludwigsburg University of Education, Germany. He worked as a secondary school teacher before starting a career at the university where he received his PhD in 2008. He is currently head of the Institute and coordinates a number of transnational projects (e.g. DIVA, proPIC, ETP, digTED@EU).
Götz Schwab has a wide range of research interests including Conversation Analysis for Second Language Acquisition (CA-SLA), Virtual Exchange/telecollaboration and the use of mobile technology, syntax, low achievers and students-at-risk, especially at secondary schools, ELT/FLT methodology in primary and secondary schools as well as Content and Language Integrated Learning (CLIL).

Chris Spurr is a trainer, educator and community development practitioner with the Northern Territory Department of Education. He specializes in working with Indigenous people to improve educational standards, provide vocational training and investigate and develop entrepreneurship opportunities. Chris has worked with communities throughout Africa and Australia.

Beverley Topaz, Ph.D., is a senior lecturer in the English Department at Kibbutzim College of Education, Tel Aviv, Israel. Her Ph.D. is in Educational Leadership from Leicester University, United Kingdom. Her research interests include initial teacher education, second career teachers, intercultural competencies, online collaborative learning, inclusive education, professional development and educational leadership.

Lalitha Tripura Sundari, a former student in the Masters in Global Education program at Charles Darwin University, holds an M.S. in I.T. and an MBA in HR, and her research interests encompass Storytelling, Intercultural studies, Indian diasporic writing, and Gender and women's studies.

Anja Vocilka holds a degree in education and is a member of both the Department of Political Science and the Institute of Social Sciences at Ludwigsburg University of Education. She is also involved as a member of the award committee for the Prize of the City of Ludwigsburg.

Tina Waldman, Ph.D., is a lecturer and researcher in the Department of English Teacher Training at Kibbutzim College of Education, Tel Aviv, Israel. Her fields of interests include applied linguistics, combining traditional approaches of language teaching with the latest developments in teaching theory, and collaborative online learning research and methodology. Her current research interests address intercultural communicative competence, a multi-disciplinary view of compassion, and social-emotional skills in teacher training. Her recent publications focus on online collaborative learning as a path to teacher's resilience and compassionate development.

Xirui Wang is a teacher and an education researcher in Australia. His main research areas are communications, education policies, and digital technologies in education.

[transcript]

PUBLISHING.
KNOWLEDGE. TOGETHER.

transcript publishing stands for a multilingual transdisciplinary programme in the social sciences and humanities. Showcasing the latest
academic research in various fields and providing cutting-edge diagno-
ses on current affairs and future perspectives, we pride ourselves in the
promotion of modern educational media beyond traditional print and
e-publishing. We facilitate digital and open publication formats that can
be tailored to the specific needs of our publication partners.

OUR SERVICES INCLUDE

- partnership-based publishing models
- Open Access publishing
- innovative digital formats: HTML, Living Handbooks,
  and more
- sustainable digital publishing with XML
- digital educational media
- diverse social media linking of all our publications

Visit us online: www.transcript-publishing.com

Find our latest catalogue at www.transcript-publishing.com/newbookspdf